GOD is ALIVE

To my cousin Janet —
May God bless you and
walk with you always.

Bill

GOD is ALIVE

BILL COMBS

Pleasant Word
A Division of WINEPRESS PUBLISHING

Printed in the United States of America

Packaged by Pleasant Word, a division of WinePress Publishing, PO Box 428, Enumclaw, WA 98022. The views expressed or implied in this work do not necessarily reflect those of Pleasant Word, a division of WinePress Publishing. Ultimate design, content, and editorial accuracy of this work are the responsibilities of the author.

Unless otherwise noted, all Scriptures are taken from the Holy Bible, New International Version, Copyright © 1973, 1978, 1984 by the International Bible Society. Used by permission of Zondervan Publishing House. The "NIV" and "New International Version" trademarks are registered in the United States Patent and Trademark Office by International Bible Society.

Scripture references marked KJV are taken from the King James Version of the Bible.

Scripture references marked NASB are taken from the New American Standard Bible, © 1960, 1963, 1968, 1971, 1972, 1973, 1975, 1977 by The Lockman Foundation. Used by permission.

ISBN 1-57921-710-9
Library of Congress Catalog Card Number: 2003107359

TABLE OF CONTENTS

"But God demonstrates his own love for us in this: While we were still sinners, Christ died for us" (Romans 5:8).

PREFACE

You picked this book up because God wanted you to. If you don't believe in God, read a page or two. He's real whether you think so or not. In our humanness we are limited; and in those limitations we neither can, nor do, know everything. Then we get into a bunch of stuff we either deny, don't understand or are afraid of. Yet, like strong medicine, we may not want to take it, but it's for our own good.

You really don't want to hear this, but yeah, it's a matter of LIFE or DEATH. YOURS. Nobody can do it for you, yet we all face it. You've got what it takes. You'll never be the same again.

If you believe in God, that's very wise. Yet neither you nor I are wise within ourselves. In fact, only by the Spirit do we seek and recognize God. It does take a choice to believe and then follow Him. That can only happen when we realize how limited we are.

So if you're a believer, what kind are you? You can have as dynamic and mature a faith as you want, as much as you'll lose yourself and get more of God. It's also our responsibility to help others see the truth of Jesus Christ in us and through us. There's also the marvelous potential that an active, aggressive faith will bring you.

I lay no claim to being a great Christian; Christian is enough for me. Read on, as brothers and sisters in Christ; we're here to help each other and glorify Him.

Scripture taken from the HOLY BIBLE, NEW INTERNATIONAL VERSION.

GOD IS ALIVE

"For though we live in the world, we do not wage war as the world does." (2 Corinthians 10:3)

There is a war between good and evil. There are absolutes. God is absolutely good and Satan is absolutely evil. Both of them want you. Whose side are you on?

Until you decide you're on God's side, you will never live up to your potential. You may do great things and accomplish marvelous achievements, but you will never be satisfied and never have peace.

You have two choices. There's no middle ground. It's either one or the other. Staying uncommitted only keeps you in the crossfire. All your life you will make moral choices. We all sin and we all screw up. It's not how much you've lost your way or stumbled, it's in the direction you're headed in. Are you struggling to God or stumbling to Satan? Is your life heading to heaven or to hell?

God is alive. God is a spirit. There are angels. There are demons. There is a devil. There is a supernatural spirit world that exists in real-time, that is parallel, and part of our physical world.

I once heard a preacher scoff at the notion that some mental illness could be demon-inspired. Indeed, he thought demons were the product, not the producers, of some mental illness. When Jesus drove the legion of demons into the herd of pigs, did He use Prozac? When Satan tempted Jesus in the desert, was He hallucinating?

What was true then is true now. We've just gotten a lot smarter, or so we think. We've grown so scientifically and technologically advanced that we're incredibly self-sufficient and self-dependent. If we can't measure it, produce it, or synthesize it, it either doesn't exist or it doesn't matter.

Just because we walked on the moon or can microwave a pizza, do you think God is impressed? He made heaven and earth. Do you think because we have heart transplants and satellite dishes that Satan packed his bags and left? No. He is the author of evil.

It's my contention that as we have advanced intellectually we have become dumber spiritually. When humans lived close to the land they had a better sense of God. A man in the Middle Ages may not always have lived in spirit and truth, but he knew that God existed. He didn't merely believe it; he knew it.

Realize how life is today. We collapse after a killer day at work or school and become slave to the TV or computer, stuffing our existence with meaningless triviality; so busy escaping, muddling through life. What do we need God for?

Heaven on earth? Not quite. The devil is laughing his tail off. There's nothing wrong with TV, the Internet, or whatever. The problem is when we immerse ourselves in so much recreational noise and are so dizzied by our own talents, we forget that we are the creation not the creator. In effect we lose ourselves in a world of our own fabrication and as we depend on ourselves and are absorbed by ourselves and things of this world, we lose focus on God and His will for us.

God made us to have spiritual, physical, and mental needs. Take care of your body. Exercise and eat right. Take care of your mind. Put good things into it and exercise it. Most importantly, take care of your soul. Put God's Word into it, invite the Holy Spirit in, recognize God as God and Jesus as Lord, then exercise your faith.

Just as your stomach growls for food and your mind reels from boredom, so too your soul longs for God. You know that gnawing feeling of incompleteness, the elusive scramble for happiness and fulfillment, indeed the meaning for your own existence? Your soul is starving for nourishment. Feed it. Exercise it. The creation longs for the Creator. The really great thing is, the Creator longs for you too.

Modern conveniences and diversions aren't bad. Don't be blinded by them. God wants you to enjoy life, but don't stay in a corner and miss the whole universe open to you. Take a break from man-made things. Refresh your perspective with God-made things.

How ardently we guard our bodies and worry over our safety, health, peace of mind, comfort, fun, etc. How diligently we vex over the temporal. Yet how strenuously do we guard our souls? You have a choice to make. It's my prayer you make the right one.

> "Do not be afraid of those who kill the body but cannot kill the soul. Rather, be afraid of the One who can destroy both soul and body in hell." (Matthew 10:28)

GOD

"Be still and know that I am God; I will be exalted among the nations, I will be exalted in the earth." (Psalm 46:10)

Everything good comes from God. Do you believe in God? Do you believe in good? Consider the natural world. Green grass, hardwood forests, mountain lakes, an ocean breeze, a fiery sunset: all are good things. So is the smell of a newborn baby, the crunch of a ripe apple, the patter of a spring rain, a mouthful of chocolate, a lungful of crisp December air. What about a child's laugh, a cop's courage, a grandfather's smile, a mother's vigilance, a friend's embrace, a nurse's compassion and the giggle of a teenage girl?

Every productive thought, every selfless deed, every compassionate act, every sunrise, leaping porpoises on a shimmering sea, puffy white clouds, a dappled gray Arabian stallion, are all from God. Everything of beauty, merit, and good comes from God. This encompasses the physical, intellectual, and spiritual world. Honor, loyalty, and integrity are all from God, so are faith, hope, and love.

You need a miracle to believe in God? Have you ever felt a baby kick? If that's not enough, consider nature. How are salmon able to return to the same spawning grounds? How does the moon know exactly how to revolve around the earth? How in the world do bears hibernate? How does your body grow? Why do stars fall from the sky? Why are veins blue in your arm but red in your eyelids?

Consider the intellectual world. Think of the polio vaccine, the airplane, the internal combustion engine, the silicon chip, the laser, the space shuttle, nuclear medicine, thermodynamics, the microscope, the microwave, the television, the telescope, music, art, and literature. Reflect on the greatness of Einstein, Da Vinci, Churchill, Mother Theresa and Shakespeare. How could the same evolutionary container come up with satellite guidance systems and the Macarena?

Consider the spiritual world. Why does doing something nice make you feel good? Why does doing something bad make you feel bad? How can you look at your lover and get all tingly and goofy? How do you sense someone looking at you when your back is turned? How can someone kill themselves? It defies logic. How can someone risk their life for someone else? Completely illogical. How can tiny Israel survive? Why has the Bible withstood the ages? How does a mother sense something wrong with her child? Why does the skin crawl on the back of your neck from an unseen threat? How have you survived the close calls and near-misses in your life? Where does the fear or anger come from when you consider God? Why the rabid disbelief from some? Why would one rail against something that doesn't exist? Why does Christmas make you cry?

Is God real? Do you have to see something to make it real? Can you see the wind? Have you ever looked at a drop of water under a microscope? With your eyes you see nothing, yet with more powerful eyes you see things you didn't see before.

If a tree falls in the forest and no one is there to hear it, does it make a sound? Of course it does. That question fairly sums up our arrogance and ignorance. If a grizzly mauls you in the wilderness and there are no witnesses, did you really scream?

Remember, we're the same bunch that thought the world was flat a few years ago. Then we discovered it was round. We're the same bunch that used to drill holes in peoples' heads to rid them of ill humours. The good folks in those days thought they were quite enlightened also. Like Clint Eastwood said in one of his movies, "A man's gotta know his limitations . . ."

Marvelous as we are, we must admit our limitations. With that being said, would you admit that there could be things beyond our capabilities to sense, to prove, to grasp? And what about the things we sense that aren't physically sensed, that aren't detected by our five senses?

"At that time Jesus, full of joy through the Holy Spirit, said, 'I praise you Father, Lord of heaven and earth, because you have hidden these things from the wise and learned, and revealed them to little children. Yes, Father, for this was your good pleasure.'" (Luke 10:21)

Now what is Jesus telling us? Could it be that if we'd never seen a tricycle and didn't have a clue what one was, that when presented with a shiny red tricycle, all of us intellectual adults would analyze, disassemble, ponder and conjecture, only to be amazed when a toddler ambles over, sits, sticks out his tongue and simply rides away. Often the ways of the Lord are foolishness to men. We try to reason everything when the simple truth is: SOME THINGS CAN'T BE REASONED and don't need to be anyway.

I have to shake my head every time I hear someone denying the reality of God, because to them a passage of Scripture doesn't make sense or can't be authenticated. Since when does the universe revolve around human reason? God doesn't need our recognition to be real.

God is the Creator. He is the author and perfecter of everything, including you and me. He put everything in order and order in everything. As His creation, we are His child. He loves us. However, He gave us free will. He gave us freedom of choice, but we have to choose. If we can admit we are limited, maybe there is reality beyond our comprehension and senses.

Maybe we need more powerful eyes.

"Now faith is being sure of what we hope for and certain of what we do not see." (Hebrews 11:1)

Do you still doubt God's existence? If you do, that question just irritated you. Why are you angry at something you don't believe in?

Look around. God is everywhere. He is the Creator, not the creation, but doesn't a masterpiece have the master's brush strokes? Then recognize Him in the stillness of the earth an hour before sunset. He's in an eagle's cry as it soars on thermal winds through a golden desert canyon. He's evident in every man, woman, and child that faces each day giving it their best. He's in a cold, clear starry night. He's in the trusting eyes of the little ones and the softened hearts of emotionally scarred adults looking for answers. He's in a friend's embrace and an old man's tears. He's in the tug of your heart when your child takes her first steps or leaves home for summer camp. He's in a cold glass of milk and a dish of fresh strawberries. He's in the faith, hope, and love that's in us all.

> "For since the creation of the world God's invisible qualities—his eternal power and divine nature—have been clearly seen, being understood from what has been made, so that men are without excuse.

> "For although they knew God, they neither glorified him as God nor gave thanks to him, but their thinking became futile and their foolish hearts were darkened. Although they claimed to be wise, they became fools. . . . They exchanged the truth of God for a lie, and worshiped and served created things rather than the Creator—who is forever praised. Amen." (Romans 1:20–22, 25)

Don't try to figure it all out. Nobody can. Open the door just a crack. A little kid eating ice cream doesn't want the recipe; he just knows it tastes good. You were a child once, you still are—God's child.

HE'S REAL. You don't have to see Him to know it even though He's all around you. He's in that feeling you just had. Ask Him to show you more.

"The God who made the world and everything in it is the Lord of heaven and earth and does not live in temples built by hands. And he is not served by human hands, as if he needed anything, because he himself gives all men life and breath and everything else. From one man he made every nation of men, that they should inhabit the whole earth; and he determined the times set for them and the exact places where they should live. God did this so that men would seek him and perhaps reach out for him and find him, though he is not far from each one of us. 'For in him we live and move and have our being.'" (Acts 17:24–28)

SATAN

"Be self-controlled and alert. Your enemy the devil prowls around like a roaring lion looking for someone to devour." (1 Peter 5:8)

Satan is real and he hates you. He hates you and everyone you love. Pick up the newspaper. A deranged mother straps her two sons in their car seats, then drowns them in a Carolina lake. A distraught teenager swallows a bottle of pills. An insane man kills his ex-wife, their kids, and then blows his brains out. A convincing lunatic persuades thirty-nine people to eat their applesauce and rendezvous with the mother ship behind the Hale-Bopp comet. An angry young man kills 168 men, women, and kids in Oklahoma, believing it was for a larger good. Two teenage boys assault their own high school with automatic weapons and homemade explosives, methodically killing and maiming their victims. Another mother takes her five children and drowns them one by one.

In the greatest nation the earth has ever seen, the divorce rate is fifty percent. People who sanction killing unborn babies would rather die than execute a convicted murderer. People who fight against the murder of unborn babies will kill adults who believe abortion is OK. This nation, founded on religious liberty, with God recognized by its founding fathers as the cornerstone and foundation of this great nation, which incorporated God into its birth and fabric, has found itself hostage to a vocal and powerful satanic minority, as these fools try to wipe away every evidence of God from American public life. They are hell-bent on removing the power behind America. The paradox is they are using freedom to squash freedom. Adams, Washington, Henry, Jefferson, and Franklin strongly believed in the personal freedom to worship God as one sees fit. The wise doctrine of separation between church and state was formed to prohibit a state religion as was the practice in European history; but it merely separates church and state and does not pit the government against the church or sanction the obliteration of Christian principles from our government. In fact, it was Washington who added the phrase "So help me God" after taking the oath of office, at which time he kissed the Bible he had his hand on. It was none other than Ben Franklin who insisted on prayer at each meeting of our founding fathers, pointing out that our fledgling nation would amount to nothing without the power of God. Read the first paragraph of the Declaration of Independence, the first amendment to the Constitution, recite our pledge of allegiance, look at the face of a penny, nickel, dime or quarter. Look at the back of a dollar bill. Amazingly, "IN GOD

WE TRUST" is as plain as day. Must drive the American Civil Liberties Union crazy. Feel free to read the writings of the founding fathers.

Now it seems we do have a state religion, which is to erase God from everything, as freedom has gone into reverse and as history is ignored and our heritage is forgotten.

"Unless the Lord builds the house, the builders labor in vain . . ." (Psalm 127:1)

Look at the world. Bosnian rape camps institutionalized the rapes of over 20,000 women. The Serbs did the same thing in Kosovo, coupled with mass murder not seen in Europe since the Holocaust. The civilized mind reels in dismay and disgust as one remembers the cry of "Never again!" The sad truth is that massacres occur every day across the globe and throughout time. Much of Africa is quite dangerous, the Middle East is always a hair-trigger, ideological madness starves its own people in North Korea. Greed and corruption do the same thing in many developing nations. A bankrupt Russia and an opportunistic China pose potential threats of global proportions. Arab terrorists flew passenger jets into the World Trade Center and the Pentagon. Courageous Americans fought back and crashed the fourth jet into a field in Pennsylvania. Flashpoints exist across the world as brother stands ready to murder brother over some lunacy or another.

A young Arab wraps himself with explosives, detonating the bomb in a Jewish market. A young Jew guns down Arabs as they pray.

Are we not all brothers? Are we not all descendants of Adam? Isn't the God of Abraham the God of Isaac and Ishmael? Isn't I AM the God of the universe? Yes, but for now Satan is the god of this world.

The Bible tells us that Satan, an archangel, rebelled against God. Indeed, he wanted to be God. As a result, Satan and a third of the angels were thrown out of heaven. You know where he landed. He hates God and all of His creation. He wants to be superior. Anything or anyone that is from God stands as a testament to Satan's inferiority.

I'm not talking bad. I'm talking pure evil. If you're misguided or mad at God and are living simply for disobedience, pleasure, and rebellion and think Satan and the dark side is cool, he'll have you killing yourself slowly or suddenly. It's only by God's hand that Satan is prevented from destroying us all, even those who worship Satan.

The devil hates everyone because people are God's creation. The more war, assault, and murder, the better he likes it. He hates the earth because it's God's creation (the same reason for you and me). The more pollution, disease, and misuse the more he likes it. He hates kindness, love, compassion, marriage, families, selflessness, and worshipping God. The list goes on and on. Anything God made, Satan wants to destroy. Anything God is for, he's against. If he can't destroy it, he wants to defile or pervert it. He wants you to have an affair, get on drugs, become a prostitute, go insane, commit suicide, rob, rape or kill.

"The thief comes only to steal and kill and destroy."
(John 10:10)

Satan loves the obvious gore, but he's a master at much subtler ways. Anger, fear, prejudice, hurt, unforgiveness, and despair are seeds he sows to harvest much more dramatic results. He knows your weaknesses. If he can't attack you through physical temptations, then be sure he'll attack your mind. He'll poison your mind with negative feelings, which he'll be sure you'll feel justified in.

The dramatic cliché of an angel on one shoulder and a devil on the other is a little simple, but true nonetheless. We all have good and evil in us. So when you hear a small, inner voice telling you to do good, it is from God. When you hear an inner voice telling you to do evil, it is from Satan.

Be warned. This is not a funny game. It's a war for your life or death. The prize is your soul. Satan doesn't want you to think long-term. He wants you to focus on right now. How can you get your quickest pleasure fix, or how can you hurt someone who's hurt you. He'll blind you a thousand different ways to the big picture.

If you were offered twenty-four hours mixed with a little intense pain, some tragedy, some pleasure, some work, some intense pleasure, and the last eight hours of sleep leading to eternal paradise; OR twenty-four hours of limitless self-gratification leading to eternity being burned in an unquenchable fire; which would you choose?

God offers the first deal, Satan the second. Granted, a lifetime is more than twenty-four hours, but what are forty, sixty, or even one hundred years compared to eternity? Too often we think of this life as an eternity, but it's not. I'm forty-five, though I feel twenty years younger mentally. Yet, I'm closer to sixty than twenty.

This life is but a whisper. Satan wants you to focus on this life only, blinding you to eternity. When you focus on this life and this world, the crosshairs are right between your eyes. When you view this life in an enlightened context, living for eternity, with God on your side and your eyes on Him, then you'll live victoriously and endure this world.

For those who've chosen the dark path and love Satan, (If you've turned from God, I'm talking to you too.) no matter what Satan gives you in this life, he does not love you. YOU'RE JUST BEING USED.

> "You belong to your father the devil, and you want to carry out your father's desire. He was a murderer from the beginning, not holding to the truth, for there is no truth in him. When he lies, he speaks his native language, for he is a liar and the father of lies." (John 8:44)

You may say that Christians are also being used. I'd agree. God does use us. He utilizes us, but "used" carries the implication that work is done without reward. I argue that God's servants are His children and are brought home to heaven. Which place do you want to call home?

We can all recognize obvious satanic traps, but what about the subtle, sometimes camouflaged ones? Unforgiveness, for example, if left inside you, is a poison that will kill and blind the bearer more often than the perpetrator.

"Make a tree good and its fruit will be good, or make a tree bad and its fruit will be bad, for a tree is recognized by its fruit." (Matthew 12:33)

So then you will know good from evil by their fruit. Remember there are only two choices. Does it lead to God or to Satan? Remember also that fruit takes time to grow. Some things you may not discern early on, but when you see the fruit you'll know what to do.

Also remember that even if something seems like it has gone sour, God never goes against His Word. Sometimes you have to uproot and destroy bad habits, bad attitudes, and bad thoughts that were blinding and crippling you. In desperate situations we often rationalize solutions that in our desperation seem right and in the eyes of men and in our plights they become quite justifiable. God sees in and beyond our circumstances. What's right never changes. It's often harder. Painfully, I know only too well it's always better.

"So I find this law at work: When I want to do good, evil is right there with me. For in my inner being I delight in God's law; but I see another law at work in the members of my body, waging war against the law of my mind and making me a prisoner of the law of sin at work within my members. What a wretched man I am! Who will rescue me from this body of death? Thanks be to God—through Jesus Christ our Lord!" (Romans 7:21–25)

A cautionary note: Satan uses people and so does God. Fruit can take time to grow. Don't flee from someone because they made you angry or insulted you. Just because Satan uses someone doesn't make them evil.

> ". . . for all have sinned and fall short of the glory of God." (Romans 3:23)

Satan is the author of sin. We're all sinners. That doesn't mean we're all evil. Simply put, we all have a mix of good and evil in us. The test is, which is in control? In which direction are we headed? I put my pants on one leg at a time just like everybody else. I'm no better than you or anybody else. We're all in the same struggle, but one that is custom-made and uniquely tailored for each of us. Therefore, decide your course. Act in an enlightened manner when you're sure of the fruit being offered you. (Remember Adam and Eve?) It wasn't sex that the serpent deceived Eve with. Satan tricked her into rebelling against God. His mission and manner are the same today.

Overwhelmed? Don't be. Do the best you can to learn God's Word. Reading and studying the Bible is spiritual Powerade. Take heart, because you have plenty of help. Jesus is the way to God and your salvation. The Holy Spirit will teach you and help you. God's angels delight in doing the Father's will. There are multitudes of people, especially in His churches, who'll be glad to help.

> "If God is for us, who can be against us?" (Romans 8:31)

"Do not be overcome by evil, but overcome evil with good." (Romans 12:21)

". . . in all these things we are more than conquerors through Him who loved us. For I am convinced that neither death nor life, neither angels nor demons, neither the present nor the future, nor any powers, neither height nor depth, nor anything else in all creation, will be able to separate us from the love of God that is in Christ Jesus our Lord." (Romans 8:37–39)

"THE GOD OF PEACE WILL SOON CRUSH Satan UNDER YOUR FEET." (Romans 16:20, emphasis added)

JESUS

"In the beginning was the Word, and the Word was with God, and the Word was God. He was with God in the beginning." (John 1:1–2)

"Then God said, 'Let us make man in our image, in our likeness . . .'" (Genesis 1:26)

Jesus is the embodiment of the Word of God. He was with God at the beginning of time.

"The Word became flesh and made his dwelling among us . . ." (John 1:14)

Jesus is the key to salvation. He is the only avenue to God.

"I am the gate; whoever enters through me will be saved." (John 10:9)

So then Jesus has been with God from the beginning. He came down from heaven to do God's will. He was to be in human form. He was to teach and to heal those who were predestined to receive this. He is the sacrificial lamb of God, sacrificed by those who were predestined to hate and crucify Him, which are really all of us in a sinful world. When this was done, a new era dawned for the world.

Jesus came and baptized with the Holy Spirit. Jesus came and taught the Word and the way more powerfully than it had ever been taught before. People marveled at His authority. He taught with authority. He healed with authority. He drove out demons with authority. How? Because He is the Word and the way.

> "I am the way and the truth and the life. No one comes to the Father except through me." (John 14:6)

When Jesus was crucified, His blood provided atonement for everyone's sin. To thoroughly understand this, read John 6:35–40. Then read the first five books of the Bible. As you'll see, Moses was the deliverer for the Jewish people, God's chosen people. Jesus is the deliverer for the world, not just the Jews, but for everyone who was predestined by God to turn to Him.

> "All that the Father gives me will come to me, and whoever comes to me I will never drive away." (John 6:37)

Jesus was born to a virgin mother, a carpenter's wife. He lived about thirty-three-and-a-half years and fulfilled countless prophecies concerning Him spanning over one thousand years before His birth. He suffered verbal abuse, rejection, Satan's temptations, betrayal, physical assault and bore it all. If you need an understanding friend, Jesus knows how you feel. Not only that, He bore the weight of the world's sin so that there would be a way of salvation for those who would turn to Him.

I've heard Jesus criticized as a wimp because He was humble, mild-mannered, and preached forgiveness. I tell you, there's never been a stronger man. What man never sinned? Jesus, like His Father, loves people but He hates sin. Read John 2:13–16 and see how He threw merchants out of the tabernacle. He could have called fire down from heaven on the men who crucified Him, but He knew it was God's will. So, He endured a terrible beating and crucifixion. Imagine: the Son of God delivered to mortals to be beaten, spat on, cursed, mocked, and laughed at. Think about it. He knew beforehand what He faced and did it anyway out of love for you and me and out of love and obedience to our Father. Now read this:

> "Do you think I came to bring peace on earth? No, I tell you, but division. From now on there will be five in one family divided against each other, three against two and two against three. They will be divided, father against son and son against father; mother against daughter and daughter against mother, mother-in-law against daughter-in-law and daughter-in-law against mother-in-law." (Luke 12:51–53)

That sound like a wimp to you? Pretty chilling stuff and it's NOT saying Jesus is against families. What it is saying is the struggle between good and evil is incredibly powerful, strong enough to turn a parent against a child or a child against his parent. Jesus isn't against families, but He is FOR GOD.

"Is not my word like fire," declares the Lord, "and like a hammer that breaks a rock in pieces?" (Jeremiah 23:29)

Jesus came to wake the world, formerly dead in sin, and to crush Satan's grip. He is the biggest catalyst for change the world has ever known. In love for this world (His creation) God sent His Son. Out of love Jesus did God's will. It is love then that conquers death and sin. Truly, love conquers all.

"For God so loved the world that he gave his one and only Son, that whoever believes in him shall not perish but have eternal life. For God did not send his Son into the world to condemn the world, but to save the world through him. Whoever believes in him is not condemned, but whoever does not believe stands condemned already because he has not believed in the name of God's one and only Son. This is the verdict: Light has come into the world, but men loved darkness instead of light because their deeds were evil. Everyone who does evil hates the light, and will not come into the light for fear that his deeds will be exposed. But whoever lives by the truth comes into the

light, so that it may be seen plainly that what he has
done has been done though God." (John 3:16–21)

So then, Jesus came to divide the world. He came to
personify and illuminate the world's choice. Some will choose
Jesus. Many will choose Satan. Imagine a shipwreck where
a thousand people of all ages and races flounder in the ocean.
Lifeboats come by with enough room for everyone. Divers
jump in to assist the drowning to safety. Many come willingly but many refuse, because they don't and won't know
the owner of the lifeboats and they perish. Shouldn't those
that will, be saved?

Jesus came to save those that will be saved. There's
enough room for everyone, but not everyone will choose it.
He came to gather the sheep who know the sound of His
voice.

". . . for the sun stopped shining. And the curtain of
the temple was torn in two." (Luke 23:45)

This happened after Jesus died, at the time of Passover.
Jesus was God's sacrificial lamb. He was the blood sacrifice
for human sin. Before Jesus died the innermost section of
the temple could only be entered by the purified priests of
the Jewish tribe of Levi. With Jesus' sacrifice, the curtain
that led to the "Holy of Holies" was torn in two. Indeed
from then on, access to God, is available to EVERYONE
THROUGH JESUS. Read Hebrews 9:6–14.

So then Jesus' life and death were completely in God's
will. He willed His Son to be the way the world could be
saved. Jesus is the WAY, the TRUTH, and the LIFE.

That of course, is the GOOD NEWS but do not be deceived. Remember, God loves you but He hates sin. Think of Jesus' sacrifice as the blood from a sacrificial lamb. At the first Passover the lamb was to be a year-old male, without defect. It's blood was smeared on the doorframes of the Hebrew homes. The meat was to be roasted with bitter herbs and eaten with bread without yeast. (Read about the Passover in Exodus if you don't understand this.) When we use the blood of the Lamb of God, His blood covers our sin. To be saved we have to be in Jesus.

> "I am the vine; you are the branches. If a man remains in me and I in him, he will bear much fruit; apart from me you can do nothing. If anyone does not remain in me, he is like a branch that is thrown away and withers; such branches are picked up, thrown into the fire and burned." (John 15:5–6)

If you don't understand that, read it again.

> "For this reason Christ is the mediator of a new covenant, that those who are called may receive the promised eternal inheritance—now that he has died as a ransom to set them free from the sins committed under the first covenant." (Hebrews 9:15)

HOLY SPIRIT

"... Do not leave Jerusalem, but wait for the gift my
Father promised, which you have heard me speak about.
For John baptized with water, but in a few days you will
be baptized with the Holy Spirit." (Acts 1:4–5)

As it is written, after Jesus was crucified He rose from
death, appearing on the third day and then appeared
over the course of forty days to His disciples. (Think
about that. He was alive the whole time, He chose to let
Himself be seen when they did. Physical laws don't apply to
God.) After they had chosen Matthias as a replacement for
Judas Iscariot, the apostles remained in Jerusalem as the Lord
commanded. On the Day of Pentecost a great sound as if a
rushing wind filled the room. Tongues of fire appeared and
rested on each of them. They were filled with the Holy Spirit
and began speaking in tongues.

Jews from every nation were there. They gathered in a
crowd utterly amazed at hearing these Galileans praising

God in many languages. Each heard his own language, yet some couldn't comprehend this, asserting the apostles were drunk. This of course, displayed God's power, but also tells us plainly that He wants every nation to hear His Word.

As we read the apostle Paul's message in 1 Corinthians chapter 12, there are many gifts of the Spirit. He lists the message of wisdom, the message of knowledge, faith, healing, miraculous powers, prophecy, the gift of discerning spirits, speaking in tongues, and the interpretation of tongues. They're different supernatural gifts imparted by the same Spirit for different kinds of service as the same God works through them.

> "And I will ask the Father, and he will give you another Counselor to be with you forever—the Spirit of truth. The world cannot accept him, because it neither sees him nor knows him. But you know him, for he lives with you and will be in you." (John 14:16–17)

> "Yet a time is coming and has now come when the true worshipers will worship the Father in spirit and truth, for they are the kind of worshipers the Father seeks. God is spirit and his worshipers must worship in spirit and in truth." (John 4:23–24)

As it is written in John 7:37–39, it was God's will to have Jesus complete His mission and only after that was God's spirit freely given. So we see that the Holy Spirit is the spirit of God. It is the Holy Spirit, who fills us and dwells within us like streams of living water. Since God is a spirit, then He fills us and works inside us. The Holy Spirit works tirelessly from within so that we worship God in spirit and in truth.

> "Don't you know that you yourselves are God's temple and that God's Spirit lives in you?" (1 Corinthians 3:16)

After we have accepted Jesus as our Lord, the Holy Spirit works to make us complete. Indeed, it is by the Spirit that we accept Jesus.

> "No, we speak of God's secret wisdom, a wisdom that has been hidden and that God destined for our glory before time began. None of the rulers of this age understood it, for if they had, they would not have crucified the Lord of glory.
> However, as it is written:
> 'No eye has seen
> no ear has heard,
> no mind has conceived
> what God has prepared for those
> who love him'
> but God has revealed it to us by his Spirit.
> The Spirit searches all things, even the deep things of God. For who among men knows the thoughts of a man except the man's spirit within him? In the same way, no one knows the thoughts of God except the Spirit of God. We have not received the spirit of the world, but the Spirit who is from God, that we may understand what God has freely given us." (1 Corinthians 2:7–12)

We see that the Holy Spirit makes God's wisdom available to us. Indeed, when Peter declared that Jesus is, "the Christ of God!", it wasn't simply Peter's knowledge, but wisdom imparted by the Spirit.

I once heard a preacher scoff at the notion that Christians couldn't understand Scripture without a learned teacher. He went on to say that to expect to have God's Word somehow supernaturally explained was nonsense.

SAY WHAT????

I agree that teachers are needed, but what wisdom they have isn't their own, but from the Spirit. God uses men and women to help each other understand the Bible and that's a good thing. However, I'll shout from the rooftops that, "YES! THE HOLY SPIRIT WILL SUPERNATURALLY TEACH YOU WHAT GOD MEANS IN HIS WORD!"

> "But the Counselor, the Holy Spirit, whom the Father will send in my name, will teach you all things and remind you of everything I have said to you." (John 14:26)

I believe Jesus meant what He said. I also know it. It's nothing short of soul-stirring to read the Bible and be enabled to understand the literal meaning, but also to have layer after layer of meaning revealed. The Holy Spirit wants you to understand God and His will. It's His job to teach you everything you need to know and help you so that God's will for your life will be realized and God therefore glorified.

"In the same way, the Spirit helps us in our weakness. We do not know what we ought to pray for, but the Spirit himself intercedes for us with groans that words cannot express. And he who searches our hearts knows the mind of the Spirit, because the Spirit intercedes for the saints in accordance with God's will." (Romans 8:26–27)

"For those God foreknew he also predestined to be conformed to the likeness of his Son, that he might be the firstborn among many brothers." (Romans 8:29)

The Holy Spirit's goal is to mold and shape us so that we become as Christ-like as possible. This means as light expels darkness, the Spirit will illuminate sin in our lives, working to minimize sin and maximize God in us.

Once you're saved, things don't stop there. Salvation is to the glory of God, but once Jesus is accepted in your heart, the Holy Spirit wants you to be all you can be in this life and the next. You've got a ticket to heaven, but what are you going to do while you're here? What will you do with the gift of life? What will you be in heaven?

"For we are God's workmanship, created in Christ Jesus to do good works, which God prepared in advance for us to do." (Ephesians 2:10)

As the Spirit sculpts us, trimming away the unusable and molding and strengthening the good, we become more and more unlike our old selves. We are new creations, putting to death our former sinful nature and are born again by the Spirit. That's not to say that those born again will not sin. It is to say (Read this carefully.) that we're no longer BOUND by sin. Neither is this a license to sin. Being born again is simply your old natural self dying and a new you emerging. Like a butterfly we emerge a transformed creature. Because we're still in this world, we're susceptible to sin. We are not bound by it and as we mature in faith any habitual sin will stop and circumstantial sin will greatly diminish. If we are not changed, then either the gospel has no power or WE haven't tapped into its power because we're holding on to our natural selves. I humbly submit that more power than we can comprehend is in the gospel, all we have to do is submit to it. So, by freely inviting the Spirit in and giving God control of our lives, we are no longer slave to sin. We're no longer bound by Satan or death. For being in Jesus we are sanctified, not gods, but ever Christ-like as the Spirit seals us. No longer bound we are new wineskins filled with new wine. No longer bound, we're headed to heaven!

"For through him we both have access to the Father by one Spirit. Consequently, you are no longer foreigners and aliens, but fellow citizens with God's people and members of God's household, built on the foundation of the apostles and prophets, with Christ Jesus himself as the chief cornerstone. In him the whole building is joined together and rises to become a holy temple in the Lord. And in him you too are being built together to become a dwelling in which God lives by his Spirit." (Ephesians 2:18–22)

Just as a good tree will bear good fruit, sow the Spirit and the Spirit will bear fruit in you.

"But the fruit of the Spirit is love, joy, peace, patience, kindness, goodness, faithfulness, gentleness and self-control . . ." (Galatians 5:22–23)

The Holy Spirit is your personal counselor, giving correct advice in every situation. The Spirit is your personal trainer, pushing you to become what God made you to be. The Spirit is God inside you, strengthening you and helping you in countless ways.

My mother was an Atlanta Braves fan. My father used to laugh at her because in any crucial situation for a Braves' batter, she would exhort the opposing pitcher to, "Give him what he needs!"

The Spirit is there to give you what you need.

"Now it is God who makes both us and you stand firm in Christ. He anointed us, set his seal of ownership on us, and put his Spirit in our hearts as a deposit, guaranteeing what is to come." (2 Corinthians 1:21–22)

THE BIBLE

"For the word of God is living and active. Sharper than any double-edged sword, it penetrates even to dividing soul and spirit, joints and marrow; it judges the thoughts and attitudes of the heart. Nothing in all creation is hidden from God's sight. Everything is uncovered and laid bare before the eyes of him to whom we must give account." (Hebrews 4:12–13)

As it is written, when Satan tempted Jesus in the desert after Jesus had fasted forty days, Satan urged Jesus to turn stones into bread.

"Jesus answered, 'It is written: Man does not live on bread alone, but on every word that comes from the mouth of God.'" (Matthew 4:4)

It is also written that Jesus is the embodied Word and the bread of life. So then the Bible is not merely pages of

43

paper and ink, nor a mere compendium of words, history, and thoughts. It is the bread of life, in which there is the power, truth, wisdom, and authority of God.

When Jesus fed the 5,000 with five loaves it was not only His supernatural power and goodness that was being displayed, He was preaching truth to the people. He was teaching them the wisdom and truth of God. The loaves fortified their bodies but the Word, the Bread of Life, embodied by Jesus himself, nourished their souls.

> "Then Jesus declared, 'I am the bread of life. He who comes to me will never go hungry, and he who believes in me will never be thirsty.'" (John 6:35)

In the Bible you'll find strength, comfort, peace, wisdom, direction and all goodness as the Spirit reveals it to you. As a literary work it consists of sixty-six books spanning thousands of years. Thirty-nine books are in the Old Testament. Twenty-seven books are in the New Testament.

It is a sweeping saga of mankind's struggle with God and God's struggle with mankind. You'll read in the Old Testament mainly of the history of the Jews. You'll read of wars, betrayals, heroes, villains, and miracles. Most importantly, the character of God will be revealed to you. The literal is true, but look deeper.

As God allowed the Jews to conquer their neighbors, they were often commanded to kill everything: men, women, and children. This wasn't because God loves a bloodbath, but because He hates sin and these people would not know God. God showed He will drive sin out of our lives.

I recall reading in Exodus about the Jews wandering in the desert. I couldn't fathom how anyone could disbelieve and disobey a God who appeared to them as a pillar of cloud by day and pillar of fire by night to guide them. Then He parted the Red Sea, swallowed Pharaoh's army and later fed them with manna and quail. Yet, in almost every difficulty they wanted to go back to Egypt or build an idol to a bull. What a stiff-necked people!

Yet are we any different? How often God has revealed Himself to me and I have disobeyed. For this I had to wander in the wilderness several times.

Through the story and truth of the Israelites, we see that God gives direction, correction, supplies our every need, and wants to gather us to Him. Read the story of the Israelites and think of your own life. You too have a choice. God will lead you if you will follow.

Read the marvelous stories of Abraham, Moses, Joshua, and Joseph. Read about Samson. Read about David and Goliath. Read about the fire inside Elijah. Read about the courage of Abigail when she saved her husband, Nabal from David's vengeance. Read about Esther, who became a queen and saved her people. Read about how the Spirit came upon David's enemy, King Saul, causing him to strip off his clothes and prophesy. Read about Daniel and the lions' den. Read about John the Baptist, Paul, the prophets, and the disciples. Read about the faithfulness of Mary and Joseph. Read about the blind being able to see and the lame able to walk.

Discover all the parallels between Moses and Jesus, as Moses embodied the Old Covenant and Jesus embodies the new. Discover the parallels between the Old Testament and the New Testament, as the old points the way to the new.

Through it all runs the common thread of God's love, God's power, and God's dominion. You see that the Spirit that is of God acted in men and women even in the Old Testament, but only by Jesus' blood sacrifice for our sin was the Spirit poured out on mankind.

Read your Bible. Pray that the Spirit will reveal its wisdom and truth. If you don't have a Bible, get one. You'll find power in His Word to overcome Satan.

> "In his right hand he held seven stars, and out of his mouth came a sharp double-edged sword. His face was like the sun shining in all its brilliance." (Revelations 1:16)

This is Jesus. The sword is the Word. Against it Satan and all the forces of hell cannot stand.

Read the Bible. Get a translation you can understand. If it makes more sense to you than all of the King James Version's *verilys* and *thees* and *thous* then that's OK. In the same way the apostles at Pentecost spoke in many tongues so that many could understand. For we should learn and live in spirit and truth without human pretense.

A WARNING: Please understand, it is written to neither add to nor take away from the Scriptures and I'm not advocating this. There are some revisions of the Bible that change its meaning. These are lies. I'm simply saying that in themselves the words are nothing, as in ourselves we are nothing; so that the same Spirit that is in the words gives meaning and life to the words and His Spirit and His Word give meaning and life to us. There is only one Truth and it is of God. The Truth is God's Word, which is Jesus. If God's

Word is in Spanish or Japanese or contemporary English, it's still the truth. It's merely translated so that all men and women can USE it. I say all this because some pastors believe the only TRUE translation is the King James, which was translated from the original Hebrew and Aramaic into old English. Many Americans struggle to understand the King James, but when they read the NIV, for example, they understand it. I would much rather have anybody READ their Bible than set it aside simply because they wrestle with the words. The words are sacred because they are God's. God breathes meaning and life into them and into us. A blue cloth-bound Bible has every bit the power of a brown leather-clad one. The same Spirit speaks through the King James, the Good News, the Thompson, the NIV and the Hebrew, Greek, and Aramaic texts. Pick a Bible you understand and read it.

"Do not merely listen to the Word, and so deceive yourselves. Do what it says. Anyone who listens to the Word but does not do what it says is like a man who looks at his face in a mirror and, after looking at himself, goes away and immediately forgets what he looks like." (James 1:22–24)

Consider that verse.

When you hear the Word you begin to see clearly and see yourself clearly. If you don't act in accordance with the Word you can't see clearly any longer. Without clear vision you can't see who you are or who you're supposed to be. Eventually you lose yourself because the you that you've become you'll no longer recognize, and the longer it takes the farther you'll drift. So later you'll forget who you really should be until you hear the Word and start obeying it.

> "The grass withers and the flowers fall, but the word of our God stands forever." (Isaiah 40:8)

Since Jesus is the embodiment of the Word of God, if we want to get closer to Jesus we GET INTO THE WORD. READ YOUR BIBLE.

BATTLEGROUND

"Therefore, since we are surrounded by such a great cloud of witnesses, let us throw off everything that hinders and the sin that so easily entangles, and let us run with perseverance the race marked out for us. Let us fix our eyes on Jesus, the author and perfecter of our faith, who for the joy set before him endured the cross, scorning its shame, and sat down at the right hand of the throne of God." (Hebrews 12:1–2)

R ead that again until you understand the importance of every word. Again, there is a war raging between good and evil on a grand scale. Think of the struggle within yourself. Think of it within your community, your state, your country. Shift to a worldview, then include the supernatural world. Now expand it along the dimension of time: past, present, and future. A magnificent arena in which we're part of the universal battle between good and evil.

"Can anyone hide in secret places so that I cannot see him?' declares the Lord. 'Do not I fill heaven and earth?'" declares the Lord. (Jeremiah 23:24)

Does the fact that nothing you and I do escapes God's knowledge make you shudder? Not only God, but a supernatural gallery watches us also. The writer of Hebrews tells us then to throw off sin so that we may fulfill God's will for us. He also implies it won't be easy, we must have perseverance. Of course Satan wants to blind us, snare us, trip us, and bind us. If you were in a fight, how easy would it be to destroy your opponent if you blinded them first? That's what Satan is a master at. As Hebrews 12:1–2 tells us, we must fix our eyes on Jesus. What Satan wants is for us to shift our focus on things of this world, so that by degrees, we wander farther and farther down the wrong path. Then, because we've shifted our focus, we're more vulnerable to the snares of sin. As we're blinded and entangled, he's really gonna open a fresh can on us. We'll become so blinded and entangled that our lives will be falling apart. In our despair, our downward spiral will continue until WE make a change.

How easy it is for our enemy to defeat us if we not only can't see clearly, but we're also actively going down the wrong path. He is a master at having us defeat ourselves, which we have to do to be defeated, because he can't capture any child of God unless we cooperate. So how much easier can it be for our enemy if we blindly wander into quicksand, off a cliff . . . or even worse, chase after fool's gold, playing right into his hand?

There was a long time in my life that I was lost except for the grace of God. Again, I believe God predestined me to be His and by His Spirit HE saved me. So was I really lost? I still had to make a choice. I still had to simply get on my knees, choose to change direction, and ask Jesus to help.

I think it started for me with religious cynicism. I grew up in church, went to Sunday School, and was baptized when I was twelve. I was an "A" student, a God-and-country boy scout; even won a citizenship award in the eighth grade. As I grew, I saw people who came to church worshipping on Sunday, but didn't live it the rest of the week. I saw people going through the motions only. I saw people every Sunday who were just that . . . people. But I didn't see how such hypocritical backseat religion was right. I believed in God, but I lost faith in religion.

"These people come near to me with their mouth and honor me with their lips, but their hearts are far from me. Their worship of me is made up only of rules taught by men. Therefore once more I will astound these people with wonder upon wonder; the wisdom of the wise will perish, the intelligence of the intelligent will vanish." (Isaiah 29:13–14)

God looks at the heart. Going through rituals that mean nothing to us doesn't please God; but see the truth: He wants us to worship Him with all our hearts and then see: with sincere seeking God will reward us.

"Jesus replied, 'Love the Lord your God with all your heart and with all your soul and with all your mind.'" (Matthew 22:37)

As I got older I saw more: Jim and Tammy Bakker and dozens of other ranting and raving preachers who seemed they couldn't live a minute longer unless you sent them all the money you had . . . immediately. So I confused the messenger with the power of truth in the message; shrugged and shifted my focus. Through the idealized eyes of youth I wrongly let the conscious misdeeds of the few blind me to the courageous diligent struggle of the many. In my disillusionment I threw the baby out with the bathwater, rationalizing that any message no better lived must not have the power it purported to have.

THE SHORTCOMINGS ARE OURS NOT GOD'S!

I don't know how many times I've attended church while I was in intentional sin. If I had cast the first stone, I would have been stoned to death a long time ago. Have I been a hypocrite? Yep. A sinner? Have mercy!

See what the enemy did? See what I let him do? Looking back, let's make one thing clear: PUT YOUR FAITH IN GOD, NOT MEN.

Only God is God. Focus on Jesus only. No man or woman can be God, and contrary to what some religions teach, God didn't start out as a man. If that were true any of us could become God. We can't, only God-like. Don't believe in anyone such that your FAITH is in them. People are people. (I'm not saying you can't trust and believe in someone in a human, relational sense.) What I am saying is: Believe with that wholehearted, fundamental, soulful, bedrock faith IN GOD, not in men or me or anybody else. Indeed, I am just like you. All I suggest is that you give God a chance. The rest is primarily between you and Him. We can help each other, but the daily relationship is for you and God to work out and enjoy.

As I said before, I put my pants on one leg at a time just like anyone else. I am a sinner, no better or worse than anyone and only by God's grace did I change direction.

After Satan worked on my mind and I lowered my sights, he tempted me with things of this world. As a teenager I started reading Playboy and Penthouse. Later, I started buying more explicit magazines and videos. Years later I had hundreds of magazines and almost that many movies. I didn't just enjoy it, I was obsessed with it.

Needless to say, this caused problems after I got married. We both had weaknesses that Satan exploited. Pornography was mine. Pornography is a window to hell. By keeping that window open, I left myself and my family open to Satan. Now none of us would expose ourselves or our families to an obvious threat, but sex sin is packaged as something deceptively and naturally desirable. Anyone who's ever fished knows that to catch fish you have to use attractive lures and many times, even hide the hooks. So there I was, swallowing the bait, not even feeling the hooks because I was swimming right to him. And I was hooked. Jesus isn't the only fisher of men.

As life hit us in other ways and due to my blindness, our marriage deteriorated. The pornography planted and nourished a powerful seed for other women. Years passed. The chinks in our armor got wider and wider and we grew farther and farther apart. When I did have an affair, I felt justified. (See how Satan blinded me, had me baited towards him, and in my ignorance I followed.) What I did was very human, but still wrong. God allows us choices and then we have to live with the consequences of our choices.

Now understand this, since we're all in this humongous war between good and evil; God and Satan; don't be fooled into thinking that since such awesomely powerful forces are at work, that we have no responsibility, no choice, and no power. It is by God's grace that we have the gate and our advocate and Savior (Jesus), and the helper (the Holy Spirit). Even though everyone who accepts Jesus was predestined to do so, it's still our choice. We can choose salvation or not and we can lose salvation.

> "If we deliberately keep on sinning after we have received the knowledge of the truth, no sacrifice for sins is left, but only a fearful expectation of judgment and of raging fire that will consume the enemies of God." (Hebrews 10:26–27)

Jesus will never cast us out, as it is written, but we can turn our backs on Him. We can choose to follow or turn away.

> "Let us not become weary in doing good, for at the proper time we will reap a harvest if we do not give up." (Galatians 6:9)

> "I am the vine; you are the branches. If a man remains in me and I in him, he will bear much fruit; apart

from me you can do nothing. If anyone does not remain in me, he is like a branch that is thrown away and withers; such branches are picked up, thrown into the fire and burned." (John 15:5–6)

So the Spirit pushes us toward God and Satan pulls us away. Surely we are influenced by both, but we all choose one or the other. The choice is the key. Once you make your choice, each side has resources designed to make you more Christ-like or more Satan-like. Do not be deceived. A person who has chosen Jesus can never be Jesus, only Christ-like. The reverse is also true. One who has chosen darkness can be evil. They can't be Satan, but they can be Satan-like. So then, there are good people and evil people.

"The mind of sinful man is death, but the mind controlled by the Spirit is life and peace; the sinful mind is hostile to God. It does not submit to God's law, nor can it do so. Those controlled by the sinful nature cannot please God.

"You, however, are controlled not by the sinful nature but by the Spirit, if the Spirit of God lives in you. And if anyone does not have the Spirit of Christ, he does not belong to Christ." (Romans 8:6–9)

God hates rebellion. Sin is rebellion against God. You can't be sinless by yourself. Only when covered by Jesus' blood will you be pure and acceptable to God. To stay in Jesus you have to first choose Him but you also have to repent of your sin and become a new you. Otherwise, it doesn't matter how much money you've given the church or what you do. If you don't accept Jesus as the Son of God and repent and stay in Jesus, when you die Jesus will say, "I don't know you." The door will be closed where there will be much wailing and gnashing of teeth.

> "Therefore, brothers, we have an obligation—but it is not to the sinful nature, to live according to it. For if you live according to the sinful nature, you will die; but if by the Spirit you put to death the misdeeds of the body, you will live, because those who are led by the Spirit of God are sons of God. For you did not receive a spirit that makes you slave again to fear, but you received the Spirit of sonship . . ." (Romans 8:12–15)

Again, when we accept Jesus we receive the Holy Spirit. When we receive the Holy Spirit we're no longer SLAVE to sin. This is open to EVERYONE. Some will choose Jesus, but many will not. By the blood of Jesus we are saved and by the Spirit we are maximized.

After the fall of the wall of Jericho, the Israelites destroyed the city, killing every living thing in it except Rahab the prostitute and her family because she helped Israel. The city's treasure was brought out and devoted to the Lord.

Then they went out to conquer the city of Ai. This time the Israelites were routed. Joshua tore off his clothes and fell face down before the ark asking God why they had suffered defeat.

Joshua found out that although Jericho's plunder had been devoted to God and forbidden to anyone, a man named

Achan had taken for himself a robe, 200 silver coins, and an article of gold. For this he and all his family were burned. Then God turned from His anger.

I recall after I had gotten rid of ALMOST all of the X-rated videos and magazines, things got better. However, I decided to keep just a few movies and a few magazines. One night the Spirit warned me to get rid of them. I ignored it and the next day, incredibly, my wife found them. I had hidden them in the basement ceiling!

> "That is why the Israelites cannot stand against their enemies; they turn their backs and run because they have been made liable to destruction. I will not be with you anymore unless you destroy whatever among you is devoted to destruction." (Joshua 7:12)

What I was doing was legal, but not right in God's eyes. When I chose to hold on to a remnant of sin, God would not put up with it. Neither you nor I can stand against our enemy if we willingly allow sin into our lives. Like the Israelites, I had to stop this or I didn't have a chance. We can't have all of God unless He has all of us.

Knowing this, I must admit it had such a powerful hold on me that even though I had finally gotten everything out of the house, I hadn't truly gotten rid of it. A friend of mine was holding the stuff for me. Maybe I was hoping God would change His mind and let me hold on to part of my old self. (He won't and He didn't.)

Ashamed as I am to say this, it must be said. A year passed after I wrote half of this book before I finally couldn't stomach it any longer, got the stuff back and threw it ALL in a dumpster. Thank God this book wasn't published three years ago. (I tried.) What kind of a witness would I be for the living Lord when I was trying to have my cake and eat it too. God doesn't play that game. I was the very same person I had always hated, a puffed-up hypocrite. A lesson I hope I've learned is: A DECISION DELAYED IS A DECISION NOT MADE!

How terrible if this book would have been published then. Of course, God blocked it and rightfully so. What had been an earnest desire to entreat others to God was doomed because I was deliberately holding on to sin. Which is to say I was deliberately holding on to self. THAT is what it all boils down to. Who is in control of your life? Better not be Satan or yourself; IT HAD BETTER BE GOD! What wouldn't we give up if HE asked us to? BETTER BE NOTHING! How much of our lives will we give to Him? BETTER BE ALL!

Understand that the Bible is our guidebook, our manual for life. God doesn't go against His Word and He doesn't want us to. If it's against His Word, it's not of God. Just as dark is contrasted by light, the Holy Spirit will reveal anything in our lives God wants us to do or not to do. Through prayer we talk to God and He will talk to us.

How miserable it is to have God chastening you and the devil trying to destroy you. I know, because I've been there. I was following God only halfway. Halfway is not good enough. It was like God had one leg; the devil had the other and they were about to make a wish. By not submitting to God I had more than one master. I served myself much of the time. I served God some of the time and Satan some of the time. Of course, if you're serving anyone other than God you're really serving Satan.

"That man should not think he will receive anything from the Lord; he is a double-minded man, unstable in all he does." (James 1:7–8)

There was also a time that for kicks I experimented with a Ouija board. Whenever I did it the indicator would very definitely, very strongly move. There was one spirit that told me she had been my wife in a previous life. (Go ahead and laugh.) She or it or whatever it was knew things that the other players had no way of knowing. Again by degrees I was led farther and farther down the wrong path.

There I was—being seduced by a demon while my life, marriage, and job all continued a steady descent. Then another spirit began appearing. It spelled out it wanted to kill me. Naturally, I insulted it in countless ways, laughing it off, even though I'd felt a profound chill go through me.

It started showing up every time I played. It kept saying it hated me and wanted to kill me. Before you laugh too hard, know this: My brother Eddie and I went on a hunting/camping trip when this was very intense. We had a blowout around a curve going almost sixty. The tire was almost new. It was ripped open but we couldn't find anything we'd hit.

Later, after sundown the batteries went out in a new flashlight when I was maybe a mile back in the woods. A powerful panic seized me as the flashlight faltered. It left only after I'd prayed. Reorienting myself, I stumbled out of the woods, exhausted, as my brother came looking for me.

That night we ate by a fire. I'd brought along the Ouija board. You can guess who showed up. It said it wanted to kill me. Of course I responded crudely in kind. I asked where it was. It answered, "I A-M H-E-R-E." That chill hit me. I saw Eddie's eyes go wide when we both heard human footsteps in the brush about forty yards away.

A squirrel scampers, a deer drags its feet, a possum or a coon rummages around. No four-legged animal walks like that. We stared at each other; put the Ouija board up and shook our heads.

We put the fire out and went to bed, figuring it'd be OK since we'd stacked bricks two feet high around it, a light rain was falling and a slight breeze was blowing the other way. Dog-tired, we dragged into the tent and collapsed.

Hours later I woke groggily to Eddie's screams. Believing it to be a dream, I sat up halfway, seeing the front of the tent gone, ringed in flames. "Man, this is weird," I mumbled as I looked down to see the foot of my sleeping bag on fire. The smell of smoke and Eddie's shouts finally made me a believer.

After beating the fire out we went back to sleep under the stars, reeking of burnt fabric. The morning light revealed how the fire had traveled a narrow path some fifty to sixty yards right to the tent.

"Let no one be found among you who sacrifices his son or daughter in the fire, who practices divination or sorcery, interprets omens, engages in witchcraft, or casts spells, or who is a medium or spiritist or who consults the dead. Anyone who does these things is detestable to the Lord, and because of these detestable practices the Lord your God will drive out those nations before you." (Deuteronomy 18:10–12)

That's pretty clear. Shoots a hole in the Psychic Friends, too. So, there was yours truly, chatting on the Cosmic Love Line with one spirit while on line two, others (or maybe the same one) wanted me dead. The cold truth of it was they both served the same master. Whether through curiosity, flirtation, or misguided machismo, they wanted me to keep the door open to the spirit world.

You've got to understand. First of all, God wants us coming to Him. He wants us to depend on Him and to develop and maintain a relationship with Him. Secondly, THERE IS A WORLD OF DECEIVERS out there. THERE ARE THOSE IN HUMAN AND SPIRIT FORM WHOSE MISSION IT IS TO LEAD US ASTRAY!

> "When men tell you to consult mediums and spirit-ists, who whisper and mutter, should not a people in-quire of their God? Why consult the dead on behalf of the living? To the law and to the testimony! If they do not speak according to this word, they have no light of dawn." (Isaiah 8:19–20)

I believe there are psychics and spirits who can tell you pieces of the future and the past. They can't tell you the whole truth because the truth is not in them. They are liars or pawns of liars.

> "And no wonder, for Satan himself masquerades as an angel of light. It is not surprising, then, if his servants masquerade as servants of righteousness. Their end will be what their actions deserve." (2 Corinthians 11:14–15)

It must also be discussed that New Age thinking is a deception. The philosophy, that anyone can do anything they want and when they die a loving God will accept them, is a lie.

God is a loving god, but He hates sin. Out of love He provided Jesus to atone for our sins. We have to accept Jesus to receive this atonement. In effect, we must believe He was, who He was, in what He came to do, and that HE IS. The Holy Spirit then moves in and changes us from the inside out. We either choose to give God our best and remain in Jesus or we don't. If you're not in Jesus when you die; you fry. It's that simple and potentially that harsh, but again I stress that salvation is simple. Give HIM a chance.

Does Satan give you a better deal?

That's the reality. The deceivers work very hard to complicate the Issue, to camouflage the truth. The deceivers want us to believe in more choices. After all, how could a loving God take His creation and chuck 'em into eternal fire? Well, it's our choice. It's a great big power struggle between good and evil; truth and lies.

> "See to it that no one takes you captive through hollow and deceptive philosophy, which depends on human tradition and the basic principles of this world rather than on Christ." (Colossians 2:8)

IF IT DOESN'T MATCH UP WITH THE WORD OF GOD, IT ISN'T FROM GOD.

As my life continued its downward spiral, my mother and father urged me to get as close to God as I could. At one time Lynda and I were on the tail-end of a seven year span which had seen a deer hit her windshield injuring her neck leading to years of pain, the deaths of our remaining grandparents, our home burglarized, my mother's first bout with cancer, her father's death, my father's death, her mother's strokes, two separations, her mother's death at Christmas, my affair, several counselors, therapists, my mom's death and an untold amount of hurt and anger between us.

I said all that, not to garner your sympathy but simply to describe the situation. As you can imagine, my stomach was shot. I had diverticulitis. I had chest pains and dizzy spells. I went for years of not sleeping more than three or four hours at night. Sciatica shot pain down both legs into my feet. My job was stressful and it was off the chart at home.

I contemplated suicide several times. The hopelessness and despair of this world smothered me, gripped me, and wouldn't let go. My parents, family, and friends kept telling me to get close to God.

I started reading the Bible again, regularly. It was 1994. My mother was hospitalized for a month after a stroke and an extensive cancer operation. Lynda's dad died a month after my mom went home. Things being what they were between her and me, she took the kids and left, going to her mother's that summer.

My older brother was getting divorced from the girl he'd married shortly after college. He asked me to visit that July 4. Over a few beers, we stared at each other, no doubt remembering each other as happy, little goofy kids; trying to reconcile our lives' unforeseen misfortunes. We talked a little about God, though not much, wishing He'd help us; wondering what in the world was taking Him so long.

The next morning we bought breakfast at McDonalds. The total came to $6.66. The cashier groaned and shuttered saying "Whoa . . . 6-6-6 . . ." A chill went through me as everything bad that I'd been involved in intentionally or unintentionally flashed through me. Kenny and I exchanged a nervous laugh.

As we arrived back at his apartment building, he punched my arm, "You think that was weird at the restaurant? Look at this!" The trip odometer on his truck read 666. He shook his head, saying he'd recently reset it.

As I drove home, stunned but strangely energized, God spoke to my Heart, my mind, telling me slowly yet firmly that Satan was real and he had been after me and my family big time.

Anger overruled any biblical knowledge I had as I returned to an empty house. That night I shouted and cursed the devil as adrenaline surged through me; the pain of my wife, my kids, our parents, brothers, sisters, and friends crashed in on me.

I stood on my hill ignorantly yelling at Satan that if it was me he was after to get his best shoes shined and come get me. About two-thirty in the morning he did. I awoke to the most paralyzing, coldest fear I've ever experienced. I could neither move nor speak. I didn't see or hear anything, but I felt it. Man, I felt it. It was like an amazingly cold vacuum had come in, absent of all hope and love, filled with fear and hate.

I've been in situations where strangers have pulled a gun on me and another time put a knife to my throat. I've never been that scared in my whole life. A little voice inside me said, "Pray." As I did, the fear (Satan) slowly retreated like a receding flood, begrudgingly giving ground.

I prayed and read the Bible until the sun came up. The Spirit led me to a Christian friend and his church where the pastor and congregation are spirit-filled. He told me I had to get rid of anything in my house God didn't want. Then I had to pray in each room claiming it for Jesus and anointing it with oil. I also put Bible verses above my doorways.

I thought this was like some weird movie or something. Then, I looked back at everything that had happened and was happening still, and through the Spirit a lot of things started making sense.

Quickly and increasingly I became more supernaturally aware. The gloves were really coming off on both sides. As I prayed in each room I would alternately feel fear then strength as the Holy Spirit pushed Satan out. The Spirit led me to the right verses to put above my doors. I made a cross with olive oil on every entrance and bedroom door, praying as I did.

Laugh or shake your head, it wasn't by my imagination that one verse just would not stay above one door. It had a bad habit of being flung across the room. I had written Matthew 4:10 on it:

> "Away from me, Satan! For it is written: 'Worship the Lord your God, and serve him only.'"

That was the verse that every time I read it and especially spoke it, the Spirit would run through me like electricity. It seemed that Satan really disliked it. I finally had to tape it to the wall. It's taped there still.

Know this: if you don't believe in what I'm telling you, start back at page one or just close the book. That's just the tip of the iceberg. Some of which I'll tell you but most I won't, because I don't want the story to be about me. It's really about us all. Be assured you'll be convinced I'm telling the truth or I'm completely off my nut. If you call yourself a Christian and think I'm nuts, do you go to church? WHY? Do you read your Bible? WHY? You may as well give it to someone else, because I'm irrelevant, but the truth of my experience is the truth of ALL of our experience. There is GOOD. There is EVIL. There are forces beyond human control. Yeah, it can be scary, but to accept and feel the fear, you have to accept and know the infinitely stronger GOD!

Needless to say, spending the night in a big house alone wasn't much fun. I'm sure creaks and shadows worked on my mind. (Recall that Satan loves to work on your mind and have you do his work for him.) However, I didn't imagine dead animals turning up in my yard or concrete angels in the garden being broken or knocked over. The really interesting part was that the Holy Spirit would warn me. He still does, but let me stress that it's not my power, but God's, and God's grace preparing me.

There's a story in the Old Testament where the king of Aram tries to capture the prophet Elisha. The Arameans were against Israel, but through the Spirit, Elisha had been telling the Israelites their every move. One morning, Elisha's servant looked out to see that the Arameans had surrounded them. Seized with fear, he confronted his master. Then Elisha prayed that the Lord would open his servant's eyes so that he could see. He did. The servant looked and saw the hills full of horses and chariots of fire all around them.

"'Don't be afraid,' the prophet answered. 'Those who are with us are more than those who are with them.'" (2 Kings 6:16)

Remember that one, and: "the one who is in you is greater than the one who is in the world." (1 John 4:4)

Anyway, the harder the devil hit me and the more bizarre things got, the more I read the Bible. At that time I still had the movies and magazines, not willing to see them for what they were. Lynda and the kids came back, but our marriage was still an exercise in hostility. I was having powerfully real nightmares and strange things continued to happen. I had visions of good and evil in broad daylight and at night. I saw ghosts and demons. I watched things move. Often I felt an evil presence and then had a crushing sensation on my chest. I was almost hurt or killed several times. Almost counts, thankfully. My health declined and then my dad died.

A week after my thirty-seventh birthday my mother called asking if I'd help take Daddy to the doctor. She said he was sleeping and wouldn't respond to her. I didn't worry because he'd always been able to sleep through a train wreck. (There were seven kids in our family.)

I drove the thirty miles over, feeling uneasy but mostly feeling sorry for myself. I found him on the floor outside the bathroom. He seemed to be asleep. He wasn't. He wasn't breathing. I shook him and slapped him. Yelling at Mama to call 911, I frantically tried mouth-to-mouth. I tried CPR harder and harder. Gathering him up I tried to make him stand but he simply slipped out of my arms. Knowing he was dead, I prayed for God to revive him, having full faith that He could, but not that He would. That's a BIG difference and it hurt.

There was my sweet mother; her husband being carted out of the house, their house. My marriage had crashed and burned, but they'd been together for forty years and still nuts about each other. I'd just read the book of Job weeks earlier. Weeks, months, years later I read it again and again to learn and try to accept one of God's hardest lessons. Satan is powerful but he can only do what God allows him to do. I don't believe Satan killed my father, but I knew he would try to exploit the shock and pain from his death. I knew Daddy was in a better place but I feared for what would happen next. I hurt for my family so terribly and I hurt for myself.

Read the book of Job. Satan was allowed to kill Job's entire family except his wife. He took away all Job's wealth, then afflicted him physically. Like us, he asked God "Why?" but he never turned his back on God.

God had set limits on Satan in Job's case. He sets limits on Satan in our cases too. To withstand Satan's attacks we must understand God is more powerful than Satan. In fact, the real lesson of Job is that come hell or high water we must keep trusting God because through hell, high water or anything and everything, GOD IS IN CONTROL. He'll use Satan's attacks to reveal His mercy, His wisdom, and His power. Then He'll use Satan's attacks for good.

"And we know that in all things God works for the good of those who love him, who have been called according to his purpose." (Romans 8:28)

It's a real head-scratcher to realize that God will allow Satan to attack you. Of course, most of the time we invite Satan in. Even then God knows what we're doing and He limits Satan. We have to realize that sometimes God will chasten us to bring us closer to Him.

"Those whom I love I rebuke and discipline. So be earnest, and repent." (Revelation 3:19)

Do any of us really think that we'd really change if He didn't chasten us? I don't know about you, but I'm as stubborn as the next guy.

Just as Elisha's servant's eyes were opened to see one of God's supernatural armies, you need to know that God and His angels are real. They do His bidding on earth and in heaven. At that time in my life I hadn't seen an angel, but I had seen them in action. Here's one example, conclude what you will, I can't explain it any other way.

The day my dad died was one of the hardest in my life. After all the bad stuff that had happened to us I was devastated that day. Only months after my father-in-law's death, this completely rocked me. My mom was just getting her strength back after recovering from an extensive cancer operation that spring. I'd been reading the Bible every day. "Lord, You mean you're gonna let my mother almost die then heal her, them take my dad?" was how I felt. I believed in my heart that somehow God would fix everything. I thought that especially since my mom had almost died, Lynda's dad did die, and all this supernatural warfare had been going on, that God would send His warrior angels in, boot Satan into the next county, straighten me out, straighten her out and do it for the longed-for-heart-warming healing for our kids, us, her mom and my mom and dad. She and I had started dating when we were fourteen. Surely the Lord would straighten everything out.

As my brothers and sisters gathered, I was in shock. When she and the kids came over, it was still so awkward and so evident that everything wasn't fixed that I started getting real mad at God. How could He allow this? It was one thing to have a run of bad luck. Everyone suffers hardship, misfortune and loss, but hadn't I been reading the Bible and praying diligently? Hadn't all of us suffered for years? And what was the deal with all the supernatural activity? (Every day.) Surely I had earned some kind of frequent flyer miles or something?

Sitting here looking back, I never dreamed years would pass and still more would happen. That night after hugging my mom, my brothers and sisters, we left for home. Lynda, reliving her own father's death, was overwhelmed. As the hurt between us was still so alive and well, she couldn't open up and release her grief for both of our fathers; it was strangling her. She was worn out and in a daze when she got behind the wheel.

I worried about her driving as I followed in my truck, but as we made it safely through town I relaxed. I looked ahead as she was in the left lane of a four-lane road. She changed to the right lane. I followed, noticing headlights approaching in my rear-view mirror. As the pickup passed me fast on my left, I watched in horror as she decided to get back into the left lane.

Recall she was still suffering from the deer accident, not to mention everything else. I saw the pickup bear down on her as she changed lanes right into it. He was going to hit her smack in the driver's side door. Seconds before impact I hit my horn mumbling, "Oh God! No!" I braced for the impact as somehow the vehicles moved HORIZONTALLY ten feet apart! Now understand, they didn't swerve and didn't move diagonally. The truck was aimed at a forty-five degree angle right into her door. At his rate of speed with their distance apart, it was physically impossible for them NOT to collide. There simply wasn't enough time or space for him not to cream her as she moved right into his path.

As it was he knocked off her side mirror but that was it. After seeing the vehicles move sideways, I knew I'd just seen a miracle. Lynda and the truck stopped. An old black man with eyes big as saucers walked over to her car in disbelief. He kept on saying, "Ma'am, are you all right? I know we hit. I know we did. I heard us hit. I don't understand it. I hit you. Are you sure you're OK?" She sat dazed and completely befuddled. She'd heard it too. She'd FELT him crash into her door, but it didn't happen.

After seeing no damage to his truck, I assured him repeatedly that we'd be OK. He couldn't believe it. Finally, he drove away. He came back three more times.

No reasoned explanation of my fatigue, mental state or whatever will ever convince me that an angel didn't push those vehicles apart. Yeah, you had to be there. I guess God let the mirror be knocked off to remind us of what almost happened.

"Elijah went before the people and said, 'How long will you waver between two opinions? If the Lord is

God, follow him, but if Baal is God, follow him.'" (1 Kings 18:21)

Read on in 1 Kings chapter 18 to see how God displayed His power. How obedient and courageous Elijah was to stand up to 450 prophets of Baal and 400 prophets of Asherah. Of course, his strength came from God. Realize that one person devoted to God isn't outnumbered even 850 to 1.

See how God blessed Israel by ending a drought after the Israelites turned to Him. How will God bless you if you turn to Him now? Maybe He'll give you your life back. Maybe you'll be one He'll use against Satan to help others. Maybe you'll help turn America back to God. Imagine how He'll bless our nation if we turn back to Him.

"If my people, who are called by my name, will humble themselves and pray and seek my face and turn from their wicked ways, then will I hear from heaven and forgive their sin and will heal their land." (2 Chronicles 7:14)

The Lord spoke this to Solomon after the temple was finished. How does it apply to us today? Who are the Lord's people who are called by His name? Christians. So if we Christians in America will humble ourselves and pray and seek God and turn from OUR sins—He's talking about US, not nonbelievers—He'll heal our land. A nation is made up of men and women. Men and women of courage, self-discipline, and filled with the fire of the Holy Spirit can go to God and HE WILL restore America.

The battle begins with you, but it doesn't end there. How can God use you if you won't yield to Him? To give God control of your life is to lose your own control, for you haven't given what you're still holding on to. This is very hard. To trust something you can't see and give it that which you deem most precious is very, very hard. That's why the decision is so marvelous and so valuable. (It's harder when we're older and our brains get in the way.)

You don't have to choose God. You can continue to be your own god or follow that king of the dunghill, Satan. (Which is really the same thing, remember?) How can we love our brothers and sisters, even ourselves and say "No" to the Truth, just to keep our own power? How can we go into battle without choosing sides?

"Do you not know that your body is a temple of the Holy Spirit, who is in you, whom you have received from God? You are not your own; you were bought at a price. Therefore honor God with your body." (1 Corinthians 6:19–20)

"Whoever tries to keep his life will lose it, and whoever loses his life will preserve it." (Luke 17:33)

"The coming of the lawless one will be in accordance with the work of Satan displayed in all kinds of counterfeit miracles, signs and wonders, and in every sort of evil that deceives those that are perishing. They perish because they refused to love the truth and so be saved. For this reason God sends them a powerful delusion so that they will believe the lie and so that all will be condemned who have not believed the truth but have delighted in wickedness." (2 Thessalonians 2:9–12)

"Do not be deceived: God cannot be mocked. A man reaps what he sows. The one who sows to please his sinful nature, from that nature will reap destruction; the one who sows to please the Spirit, from the Spirit will reap eternal life." (Galatians 6:7–8)

Our mission is not to fight Satan but to be FOR GOD! By living holy lives and standing firm in whatever God has called us to do, we're fighting evil. Be sure that Satan will come against you when you step out of the crowd and by the Spirit change your life. By the blood of Jesus and its power you will have divine protection and the strength to stand.

THE CROSSROADS

"Stand at the crossroads and look; ask for the ancient paths, ask where the good way is, and walk in it, and you will find rest for your souls." (Jeremiah 6:16)

"Dear friends, do not believe every spirit, but test the spirits to see whether they are from God, because many false prophets have gone out into the world. This is how you can recognize the spirit of God: Every spirit that acknowledges that Jesus Christ has come in the flesh is from God, but every spirit that does not acknowledge Jesus is not from God. This is the spirit of the antichrist, which you have heard is coming and even now is in the world." (1 John 4:1–3)

What are you thinking right now? What's in your heart? Is God tugging at your heart, but your mind is screaming at you not to listen? Are you arguing with God about why He didn't do this or why He allowed that?

I talked to a truck driver once who had three kids. The oldest, a boy, was healthy and seemed to be doing OK. The second, a teenage son, was blind and couldn't walk. I started to say he's confined to a wheelchair, but he's not. Thanks to God, loving parents, family and friends, and his own inner fire, he's on his school's wrestling team, busy with his computer and sounds like a great kid.

The story doesn't end there. The boy has an extremely rare genetic disease. A while back they learned their youngest, a daughter, has it too. She's now blind and can't walk. I didn't see self-pity in their daddy's eyes. I saw hurt; more than that I saw pride and faith. In talking about his kids, he was so proud of them. I can only imagine the tears he and his wife have cried. Here was a strong man resolutely proud of his family. He didn't talk about faith; didn't have to. He was living it. Then he told me something else.

With his kids' medical problems his family had put in a lot of time in several hospitals: Johns Hopkins, Emory, and St. Jude to name a few. During one stay he met a little girl. About eight or nine, she was blind too.

She didn't share that terrible disease. She had burn scars over her entire body. Her dad liked to smoke cigars. He was also into drugs and drinking. He had a nasty habit of burning her with his cigar. She didn't have eyelids anymore and couldn't see because he'd burned her there, too.

He went on to say that doctors had given her new eyes and she could see a little now. He also said that no matter how rough you have it seems somebody's got it rougher.

Maybe you've lost loved ones. Maybe you've been raped, abused, divorced, or assaulted. Maybe you or a loved one has cancer. Maybe you or someone you love is hooked on drugs, has emotional problems, or has been injured.

Five years ago my mother died from her second battle with cancer. I started to say she lost her battle but that's not true. Before she was diagnosed she prayed and told me she thought God had told her whatever it was; it would be OK. I prayed too, but I felt Him say it was serious. I asked Him to give her ten more years. She told me that she too had prayed that whatever happened to please give her ten more years. As she said it, I felt electricity shoot through me and I took that for confirmation.

A CT scan led to a biopsy which led to the knowledge she had an inoperable fast-growing virtually untreatable cancer on her thyroid which had already invaded and entangled her windpipe. A tracheostomy was done and we settled into the routine of radiation, chemotherapy, and hospice.

If faith can move a mountain, then anything was possible for my mother. (She used to wear a necklace with a mustard seed pendant.) Of course, you know me. With every bit of bad news I'd just see things stacking up in God's favor. Like my dad's death, I had full faith God could heal her but unlike that time, this time I knew He would.

My brother Eddie and sister Caroline did the lion's share of the work. He lived there, tending to her at night while she came during the days. And we all watched as a sweet lady endured writing instead of talking, motioning instead of speaking, yet still doing as much as she could for herself and others. We all watched as weeks turned into months, through gains and setbacks, as she and every one of us exercised our faith.

As she grew worse she would ask if we still believed in her miracle. Once with several people in the room I felt the Spirit on me. In the corner of the room an angel stood. I didn't look higher than its chest; I didn't have to. I didn't think I was supposed to, but I did see a brilliant white, winged angel. I was at once scared and thrilled. Meekly, I asked the Lord if the angel was there to take our mother. The Lord said, "No." I of course took that to mean her miracle was at hand and told her so.

Mama got her miracle. She was healed in death. She never lost her battle. I never saw her defeated or give up. The angel was there to help all of us.

I'm sitting here rewriting over five years after my mom died. My younger brother, Neal, died over three years ago, leaving a wife and three beautiful girls. Lynda and I have been divorced for over five years now. I can hear the critics, "Hey bonehead! Where was your God then? He didn't save your father, your mother, your brother or your marriage. Wise up you knucklehead!" Well, He did save my father, mother and brother and I imagine they're doing just fine in heaven. He's guided us through all of life's storms. My wonderful, resilient kids are doing well and God introduced me to Annie, a thoroughly fabulous woman with a gentle spirit and a captivating laugh who reads me instantly and lovingly keeps me on track. We've been married over three years now.

Bizarre things still happen, though not as often, and I ask God just like you do, "Why God? Why?" I, like you, am just a fellow traveler through this adventure called life. I don't have a monopoly on misery and neither do you. It's spread around pretty well.

So again, why God? Why do teenagers have to die in car crashes? Why do adults molest little kids? Why is there cancer, cerebral palsy, muscular dystrophy and AIDS? Why are there drive-by shootings and murderous holdups for a day's wages? Why is there war and torture, greed, pestilence, hate, and prejudice? And why did you let that monster burn that little girls eyes out?

Before we get an answer we often assume there isn't an answer. Then we go on and assume there isn't a God, He just doesn't care, or whose side is He on anyway? From there we move on to say that since I don't understand You or agree with You, I will not recognize You or submit to You. You haven't protected me, my family, or the world from harm, (If we only knew everything He does!) so either You don't exist or You've turned Your back on us.

What we're really saying is: God, since I'm hurt, scared, and confused, I can't believe in You. WHOSE JOB IS IT TO HURT, SCARE, AND CONFUSE US? Then we say: God since You don't do what I want You to do, let me know when You change Your mind.

"Who is this that darkens my counsel with words without knowledge? Brace yourself like a man; I will question you, and you shall answer me.

"Where were you when I laid the earth's foundation?" (Job 38:2–4)

Understand the relationship.

"I am the Lord, and there is no other. I form the light and create darkness. I bring prosperity and create disaster; I, the Lord, do all these things . . ." (Isaiah 45:6–7)

Satan burned that little girl's eyes and did every evil under the sun. I believe God allowed it also.

Now think. Think hard. Your mind is racing in opposition to your heart. If you're tough and analytical. Here it is straight and brutally cold: Who are we to question God? He uses Satan's evil for good. We've only two choices. One leads to eternal life. One leads to eternal punishment. So make a choice.

For those more philosophical, tenderhearted types like me: How could a loving, omnipotent God let us experience pain?

"See I have refined you, though not as silver; I have tested you in the furnace of affliction." (Isaiah 48:10)

What strength, faith, character, gratitude, perspective, or love would any of us have or demonstrate if we always got our way? Think of something you've earned from sweat, prayers, and tears. How much more precious is that achievement because it cost you something? To have a deeper faith it must be used. Kind of like the oyster and the pearl; there has to be a grain of sand as an irritant for the pearl to be formed. For us to grow as Christians and to mature as adults, the trials in our lives strengthen us. Courage, for instance, can't be exercised or even defined without adversity.

"For my thoughts are not your thoughts, neither are your ways my ways," declares the Lord. "As the heavens are higher than the earth, so are my ways higher than your ways and my thoughts than your thoughts. As the rain and the snow come down from heaven, and do not return to it without watering the earth and making it bud and flourish, so that it yields seed for the sower and bread for the eater, so is my word that goes out from my mouth: It will not return empty, but will accomplish what I desire and achieve the purpose for which I sent it." (Isaiah 55:8–11)

"But he said to me 'My grace is sufficient for you, for my power is made perfect in weakness . . .'" (2 Corinthians 12:9)

Again, we are the creation not the Creator. We are strengthened by trials in our faith and character because when we realize WE can't fix what's going on and when we DEPEND ON GOD, HIS POWER is manifested in our lives. The grace HE GIVES us the WORLD SEES, and it LIFTS US UP and KEEPS US GOING, and STRENGTHENS us in the wee hours of the night and ENERGIZES us in the fray of battle, REMINDING US THAT OUR HELP COMES FROM THE LORD THE MAKER OF HEAVEN AND EARTH!

(Deep Breath . . .) Could we intellectually entertain the notion that our earthly suffering, no matter how severe, is for a purpose and pales in comparison to the peace and beauty of heaven? It's a tough thing to look beyond your circumstances when your whole life is crumbling around you, but I humbly submit that one reason we're here is to help each other while we're here and through the Spirit get out of here to heaven. So through the mud, blood, and tears we get spiritually stronger if we yield to God and become more and more useable to our brothers and sisters as we let the Holy Spirit work through us. The more adversity we face the more we realize our weakness and His strength.

"I consider that our present sufferings are not worth comparing with the glory that will be revealed in us." (Romans 8:18)

What is DEATH when DEATH has been defeated? What is SIN when we are no longer bound by it? What are DISEASE, ABUSE, FEAR, ANGER, EVIL, DESPAIR, AND INJURY where they no longer exist?

I'm not suggesting that physical pain and mental anguish aren't real. They're terribly real. What I am urging is that we look at LIFE in a different perspective. This life is only a preparation, a stopover, for eternity.

"Therefore we do not lose heart. Though outwardly we are wasting away, yet inwardly we are being renewed day by day. For our light and momentary troubles are achieving for us an eternal glory that far outweighs them all. So we fix our eyes not on what is seen, but on what is unseen. For what is seen is temporary, but what is unseen is eternal." (2 Corinthians 4:16–18)

So we stand at a crossroads. It's your choice. Do you take the popular road with Satan's mirage beckoning deceitfully on the horizon? Or do you take the road less traveled where a simple shepherd waits patiently calling your name?

If His voice is familiar to you, there is no reason, no reason at all, not to follow Him. Have you reached the blessed point of brokenness where you finally realize you need God? Follow and He'll give you what you need.

Pray and ask Jesus to be Lord of your life. Don't put it off. If you feel it, now is the time. There's no set formula. In your own words, out of your own heart, ask Jesus to help you, forgive you and be your Lord. Pray this if you wish:

Father, I am a sinner. I believe Jesus is Your son and died on the cross for me. Wash me clean Father, and bring me home. Help me to repent of my sins. Come into my heart Jesus and make me new. I turn my life over to You. May Your Holy Spirit strengthen me and guide me. Use me as You will. Amen.

> "You will go out in joy and be led forth in peace; the mountains and hills will burst into song before you, and all the trees of the field will clap their hands." (Isaiah 55:12)

If you still doubt unseen things, you know the wind is real, though you can't see it. You can see its effects as trees sway, leaves rustle, and dust swirls. So as the unseen causes visible results, good and evil in the world have (for now) invisible sources. These unseen sources are very real.

> "Seek the Lord while he may be found; call on him when he is near. Let the wicked forsake his way and the evil man his thoughts. Let him turn to the Lord, and he

will have mercy on him, and to our God, for he will freely pardon." (Isaiah 55:6–7)

"Although the Lord gives you the bread of adversity and the water of affliction, your teachers will be hidden no more; with your own eyes you will see them. Whether you turn to the right or to the left, your ears will hear a voice behind you, saying, 'This is the way; walk in it.'" (Isaiah 30:20–21)

"So do not fear, for I am with you; do not be dismayed, for I am your God. I will strengthen you and help you; I will uphold you with my righteous right hand." (Isaiah 41:10)

END TIMES

"And afterward, I will pour out my Spirit on all people. Your sons and daughters will prophesy, your old men will dream dreams, your young men will see visions.

"Even on my servants, both men and women. I will pour out my Spirit in those days. I will show wonders in the heavens and on the earth, blood and fire and billows of smoke.

"The sun will be turned to darkness and the moon to blood before the coming of the great and dreadful day of the Lord.

"And everyone who calls on the name of the Lord will be saved; for on Mount Zion and in Jerusalem there will be deliverance, as the Lord has said, among the survivors whom the Lord calls." (Joel 2:28–32)

As it is written no man knows the day or hour of the day of the coming of the Lord. It is also written that just as a woman about to give birth suffers labor pains, so will the earth as it prepares to receive the Lord.

I realize critics will say that I write this to pressure and scare some to receive Jesus. The fact that the Lord will reclaim this earth is a promise from God. In my effort to conscientiously inform you of your choices, I'd be totally wrong to omit this. This truth also points out that although God is a God of love; He is also a God of justice.

"The arrogance of man will be brought low and the pride of men humbled; the Lord alone will be exalted in that day, and the idols will totally disappear." (Isaiah 2:17–18)

"Stop trusting in man, who has but a breath in his nostrils. Of what account is he?" (Isaiah 2:22)

It is my belief that little ones today will not grow old before the Lord returns. Read the Bible, look at the world, and see what you think.

"But mark this: There will be terrible times in the last days. People will be lovers of themselves, lovers of money, boastful, proud, abusive, disobedient to their parents, ungrateful, unholy, without love, unforgiving, slanderous, without self-control, brutal, not lovers of the good, treacherous, rash, conceited, lovers of pleasure rather than lovers of God—having a form of godliness but denying its power . . ." (2 Timothy 3:1–5)

"But, dear friends, remember what the apostles of our Lord Jesus Christ foretold. They said to you, 'In the last times there will be scoffers who will follow their own ungodly desires.' These are the men who divide you, who follow mere natural instincts and do not have the Spirit." (Jude 1:17–19)

If a volcano was about to erupt and many knew this, shouldn't we warn those who don't see it? Though I don't know the time of the eruption, I see the mountain well-formed. I feel the ground rumbling and the pressure building. My intention is not to terrify but to inform. I too have passed street corners where strange-looking men screamed at all within earshot to repent or we're all going to hell. I thought they were a bunch of nuts too. Yet, don't look to men, look to God. God tells us that we're all sinners and need to repent. Looks like those guys were right about that. Thankfully, that's not the whole story. God tells us to believe in Jesus, His Son, and that Jesus atoned for our sins. Through Him we're sons and daughters of God and will go to heaven.

So the truth is both terrible and marvelous. Get close to God. Maximize your life now and insure your life forever. This is a promise of God. It will happen. In His time, when all the conditions are met and pieces in place, it will happen.

Here I go again. I must tell you that three times I felt the Spirit on me and three times I saw the same thing. Each time I looked up and saw Jesus on a white horse coming in the clouds followed by a multitude of riders also clothed in white and on white horses. The difference was that each time Jesus was markedly closer.

Was this my imagination? I know it wasn't and you do too. The feeling you had just go through you proves it. Let those who have ears, hear and those that have eyes, see. Let those who will be warned gain wisdom and prepare. What man or woman knows the day of their death or the Day of the Lord? Seek the Lord while He may be found.

"In that day the Lord will punish the powers in the heavens above and the kings on the earth below. They will be herded together like prisoners bound in a dungeon; they will be shut up in prison and be punished after many days. The moon will be abashed, the sun ashamed; for the Lord Almighty will reign on Mount Zion and in Jerusalem . . ." (Isaiah 24:21–23)

Remember the story of Abraham and Isaac, how Abraham was going to sacrifice his only son, but after his obedience and faith were established God mercifully stopped him? Imagine how tortured he felt at the thought of harming the son he loved so much. For us, God watched as His Son was ridiculed, betrayed, beaten, spat on, and had spikes hammered through Him. That's how much He loves us: to allow that to happen and Jesus to endure it. You can believe He remembers. Read the parable of the owner of the vineyard who sends his son after the tenants beat and killed his servants, and then even killed his son also (Matthew 21:33–43). How much clearer can God be?

As I was riding in on the Metro on my way to the 1997 Promise Keepers rally in Washington D.C., I saw a picture of a little Algerian boy in the paper. The article described the violence and political unrest of his nation. The photo was a close-up. He'd been dumped in a well; his throat cut. My son was ten at the time. I couldn't help it. I started crying. You had better believe God is sick of His children being robbed, raped, and killed. We all had better believe that God will not let this evil stand. Not what happened to His Son or any of His children. Our salvation didn't come cheaply. Turning our back on it is the same thing as spitting on Jesus again. We did it the first time because His sacrifice was for us all. He's given us a second chance. Don't do it again.

God is waiting. He's waiting on you. He's waiting on you to make your choice. He's waiting on you so He can use you to help others see their choice. He's waiting on you to come home.

> "Now what I am commanding you today is not difficult for you or beyond your reach. It is not up in heaven, so that you have to ask, 'Who will ascend into heaven to get it and proclaim it to us so that we may obey it?' Nor is it beyond the sea, so that you have to ask, 'Who will cross the sea to get it and proclaim it to us so we may obey it?' No, the word is very near you; it is in your mouth and in your heart so you may obey it.
>
> "See, I set before you today life and prosperity, death and destruction. For I command you today to love the Lord your God, to walk in his ways, and to keep his commands, decrees and laws; then you will live and increase, and the Lord your God will bless you . . ." (Deuteronomy 30:11–16)

Israel was reestablished in 1948. Everything I read in the Bible and from Christians who've studied the Bible says that God's time clock for prophecy runs when the Jews are in their homeland. So Israel became a nation again in 1948, but then Jerusalem was divided into sectors of control. Jerusalem didn't come under total Israeli control until 1967.

Jesus was talking with His disciples when they asked: "Tell us," they said, "when will this happen, and what will be the sign of your coming and of the end of the age?"

Jesus answered: "Watch out that no one deceives you. For many will come in my name, claiming, 'I am the Christ,' and will deceive many. You will hear of wars and rumors of wars, but see to it that you are not alarmed. Such things must happen, but the end is still to come. Nation will rise against nation, and kingdom against kingdom. There will be famines and earthquakes in various places. All these are the beginning of birth pains." (Matthew 24:3–8)

Jesus continued: "At that time if anyone says to you, 'Look here is the Christ!' or, 'There he is!' do not believe it. For false Christs and false prophets will appear and perform great signs and miracles to deceive even the elect—if that were possible. See, I have told you ahead of time.

"So if anyone tells you, 'There he is, out in the desert,' do not go out; or, 'Here he is, in the inner rooms,' do not believe it. For as lightning that comes from the east is visible even in the west, so will be the coming of the Son of Man." (Matthew 24:23–27)

Jesus is telling us not to believe it's really Him no matter how impressive someone is because He's telling us the way He'll come; everybody's going to see it. It will be so fantastic and marvelous there'll be no guessing:

> "At that time the sign of the Son of Man will appear in the sky, and all the nations of the earth will mourn. They will see the Son of Man coming on the clouds of the sky with power and great glory. And he will send his angels with a loud trumpet call, and they will gather his elect from the four winds, from one end of the heavens to the other." (Matthew 24:30–31)

And that's when the children of God are called up into the air.

Jesus continued with His disciples and here is where I believe He's talking about Israel:

> "Now learn this lesson from the fig tree: As soon as its twigs get tender and its leaves come out, you know that summer is near. Even so, when you see all these things, you know that it is near, right at the door. I tell you the truth, this generation will certainly not pass away until all these things have happened." (Matthew 24:32–34)

It could be that Jesus was simply using a natural metaphor to say that one thing points to another, but I think it's deeper than that. When He talks about the generation and the fig tree I believe He's talking about Israel. Israel is an ancient country, reborn in 1948. I believe that Israel is the fig tree and that generation won't pass away before the Day of the Lord.

I must admit I'm over a barrel whether the prophetic clock started again in 1948 or 1967; my heart says 1948. It is also true that I don't know the day, the hour, or the year. All I know is what God says and what He's shown me and others and I believe it's close.

> "No one knows about that day or hour, not even the angels in heaven, nor the Son, but only the Father. As it was in the days of Noah, so it will be at the coming of the Son of Man. For in the days before the flood, people were eating and drinking, marrying and giving in marriage, up to the day Noah entered the ark; and they knew nothing about what would happen until the flood came and took them all away. That is how it will be at the coming of the Son of Man." (Matthew 24:36–39)

So when I looked in the sky and saw Jesus coming in the clouds, why did I see that? I felt the Spirit strongly each time and I saw the same thing three times, but markedly closer each time. I think God showed me something so I could tell you about it and I believe He's simply saying, "This is close and getting closer." He wants to gather all His children and for us to be ready.

> "Therefore keep watch, because you do not know on what day your Lord will come. . . . So you also must be ready because the Son of Man will come at an hour when you do not expect him." (Matthew 24:42 and 44)

> "I saw heaven standing open and there before me was a white horse, whose rider is called Faithful and True.

With justice he judges and makes war. His eyes are like blazing fire, and on his head are many crowns. He has a name written on him that no one knows but he himself. He is dressed in a robe dipped in blood, and his name is the Word of God. The armies of heaven were following him, riding on white horses and dressed in fine linen, white and clean." (Revelation 19:11–14)

Take care of your mind, body, and soul. Get a Bible, read it, and pray. Find a church that preaches and teaches the Bible. Beware of any teaching that doesn't preach Jesus as the key to salvation and truth out of the Bible. The rest are liars. Be careful around anyone or any church where lives aren't changed and the Holy Spirit isn't welcome. I tell you, JESUS CHANGES LIVES! The flesh will make us stumble, but when people are led by the Spirit they're different and you'll know it.

Beware of many popular religions that take bits and pieces of the truth, then incorporate their own strange beliefs. I received a pamphlet the other day from the Jehovah's Witnesses. I think many of their followers are fine people but some of what they espouse is just plain wrong. For instance, they teach that the 144,000 people that go to heaven out of the Tribulation are all Jehovah's Witnesses. The Bible clearly says the 144,000 are all saved Jews; 12,000 from each of the twelve tribes from Israel (Revelation 7). They teach that it is wrong to receive a blood transfusion even to save a life. While God clearly and repeatedly says that blood is special (Leviticus 17:11) He tells us over and over again we should love our neighbor, which I would think saving their life falls into that category. This legalistic view of blood being so sacred you can't use it to help people smacks of the Pharisees criticizing Jesus for healing on the Sabbath (Luke 13:10–17). They also don't believe in celebrating birthdays (poor kids), Christmas, or the cross, saying that Jesus died on a pole. I'm sure that comes as a surprise to the disciples. See the New Testament or merely John 19:17–25, (just in these verses: Cross-3, Pole-0). They also don't believe in the Trinity, you know Father, Son and Holy Ghost separate but also ONE. I disagree profoundly with that. For example, "In the beginning was the Word and the Word was with God and the Word was God" (John 1:1). Who is the Word? Jesus, right? So here we have the Bible saying Jesus is separate, but one with God and, that the Spirit is too. See the New Testament, or John 14, 1 Corinthians 2 to see the Spirit is separate but also from God. How about:

> "Then Jesus came to them and said, 'All authority in heaven and on earth has been given to me. Therefore go and make disciples of all nations, baptizing them in the name of the Father and of the Son and of the Holy Spirit . . .'" (Matthew 28:18–19)

I figure Jesus ought to know.

I don't mean to be picking on the Jehovah's Witnesses. The point is that anybody or any group that tells you something that is against the Bible and has their own version of the Bible, you better be careful. The Bible itself says don't take away or add to it (Revelation 22:18–19). Be very suspicious if any group only lets their leader read the Bible and no one else can even have a Bible. I tell you the truth; each one of us came into this world alone and will go out alone.

Each one of us has to work out our own salvation and to do that we individually have to accept Jesus. After that, God tells us to come to Him, to pray, to learn His Word and be discerners of the TRUTH. Of course it's good and right to go to church and meet in groups of a few or thousands, but WE have to arm ourselves with knowledge so we won't be led astray and be ineffective or at worst a liability to Jesus. So the simple admonition is the sum of this book. God is Alive. There is good and evil. Jesus is the ONLY way to God. God, Jesus, and the Holy Spirit equip us and help us to fulfill His purpose for our lives. The Bible is our guidebook. The Spirit within us lights our path. God loves the sinner, but hates the sin. If we are in Jesus when we die or when He returns we're going to heaven. Jesus is coming back. We need to be ready. We can help others while we're here.

"Behold, I am coming soon! My reward is with me and I will give to everyone according to what he has done. I am the Alpha and the Omega, the First and the Last, the Beginning and the End.

"Blessed are those who wash their robes, that they may have the right to the tree of life and may go through the gates into the city. Outside are the dogs, those who practice magic arts, the sexually immoral, the murderers, the idolaters and everyone who loves and practices falsehood." (Revelation 22:12–15)

A WARNING TO CHRISTIANS

"Do not love the world or anything in the world. If anyone loves the world, the love of the Father is not in him. For everything in the world—the cravings of sinful man, the lust of his eyes and the boasting of what he has and does—comes not from the Father but from the world. The world and its desires pass away, but the man who does the will of God lives forever." (1 John 2:15–17)

"Do not conform any longer to the pattern of this world, but be transformed by the renewing of your mind. Then you will be able to test and approve what God's will is—his good, pleasing and perfect will." (Romans 12:2)

We can't be saved and be the same as we were before. The kingdom of God is about power. Power to change lives. Power to heal. Power to break the bonds of sin. Power to change hearts and minds and attitudes. JESUS changes people. JESUS changes our hearts and renews our minds. Satan will fight to keep his hold on our hearts and minds.

I write this speaking to myself as well as all Christians. Just as Satan tempted Jesus with worldly power and worldly riches and desire (Matthew 4:3–11), Satan does the same to us.

"Not everyone who says to me, 'Lord, Lord' will enter the kingdom of heaven, but only he who does the will of my Father who is in heaven." (Matthew 7:21)

Therefore we can't be the same sinners we used to be. Christians still sin, but the addictions and habits of sin that we had before we were saved must be ever broken and ultimately killed. So that the patterns of sin are reduced and strangled, so that finally we are dead to them. We would be greatly mistaken to think because we have salvation that we have a "Get Out of Hell Free" card and continue to cheat our brothers, do drugs, have affairs, lie, steal, wallow in pornography, etc. Salvation is free but it's NOT cheap! It comes at the cost of our Lord's blood and remains under our continued status with God.

"For if God did not spare the angels when they sinned, but sent them to hell . . ." (2 Peter 2:4)

". . . for a man is a slave to whatever has mastered him. If they have escaped the corruption of the world by knowing our Lord and Savior Jesus Christ and are again entangled in it and overcome, they are worse off at the end than they were at the beginning. It would have been better for them not to have known the way of righteousness, than to have known it and then to turn their backs on the sacred command that was passed on to them. Of them the proverbs are true: 'A dog returns to its vomit' . . ." (2 Peter 2:19–22)

"No one who lives in him keeps on sinning. No one who continues to sin has either seen him or knows him.

"Dear children do not let anyone lead you astray. He who does what is right is righteous, just as he is righteous. He who does what is sinful is of the devil, because the devil has been sinning from the beginning. The reason the Son of God appeared was to destroy the devil's work. No one who is born of God will continue to sin, because God's seed remains in him; he cannot go on sinning, because he has been born of God. This is how we know who the children of God are and who the children of the devil are: Anyone who does not do what is right is not a child of God; nor is anyone who does not love his brother." (1 John 3:6–10)

That seems straight up to me. God helps us by renewing our minds, by changing us. In my past, I'd slobber like a dog to look at a skin magazine or X-rated video. He changed me, so when I was tempted early on I wouldn't give in on the first time or dozen, but then I would and He'd sear my conscience. I felt so guilty because now my eyes were open and I knew I was disappointing God. (Remember how Adam felt after eating the forbidden fruit?) As time went on my appetite changed. I no longer craved pornography. Jesus breaks the bonds of sin. Thanks be to Him that stuff controls me no longer and I'm no longer slave to it. Satan is not going to attack us at our strongest points. The thief looks for weak spots. He knows mine and he knows yours. He wants to destroy us. My point: God sent Jesus to reconcile His children to Himself. He chooses to use us to be a light to the world. Don't believe Satan's lies, that a Christian can do as he or she pleases. That's a contradiction in terms, because a Christian will try to do what he or she can to please God.

Another of Satan's lies is that Jesus isn't coming back. I was shocked to hear that a majority of American clergy at some conference thought the Second Coming was a fable, just a nice Bible story. Funny, I thought the Bible was God's inspired Word.

"First of all, you must understand that in the last days scoffers will come, scoffing and following their own evil desires. They will say, 'Where is this 'coming' he promised? Ever since our fathers died, everything goes on as it has since the beginning of creation.' But they deliberately forget that long ago by God's word the heavens existed and the earth was formed out of water and by water. By these waters also the world of that time was deluged and destroyed. By the same word the present heavens and earth are reserved for fire, being kept for the day of judgment and destruction of ungodly men.

"But do not forget this one thing, dear friends: With the Lord a day is like a thousand years, and a thousand years are like a day. The Lord is not slow in keeping his promise, as some understand slowness. He is patient with you, not wanting anyone to perish, but everyone to come to repentance.

"But the day of the Lord will come like a thief. The heavens will disappear with a roar; the elements will be destroyed by fire, and the earth and everything in it will be laid bare.

"Since everything will be destroyed in this way, what kind of people ought you to be? You ought to live holy and godly lives as you look forward to the day of God and speed its coming . . ." (2 Peter 3:3–12)

This WILL happen, not because I say so. Who am I that I should be listened to? GOD says so. Just as with everything that is said by men, match whatever I and others say with the Bible. I am human and I make mistakes; every preacher and teacher is human also, but BEWARE of anybody, MAN or WOMAN or SPIRIT who speaks against the Bible. And yes, we're supposed to do our own homework and know better. Remember Jesus is the embodiment of the Word. If you want to know Jesus, get to know the Word. He gave us the Bible and preserved it for us to read and learn from it so we're not merely drones, but truly Christian soldiers.

"For certain men whose condemnation was written about long ago have secretly slipped in among you. They are godless men, who change the grace of our God into a license for immorality and deny Jesus Christ our only Sovereign and Lord.

"Though you already know all this, I want to remind you that the Lord delivered his people out of Egypt, but

later destroyed those who did not believe. And the angels who did not keep their positions of authority but
abandoned their own home—these he has kept in darkness, bound with everlasting chains for judgment on the
great Day. In a similar way, Sodom and Gomorrah and
the surrounding towns gave themselves up to sexual immorality and perversion. They serve as an example of
those who suffer the punishment of eternal fire.

"In the very same way, these dreamers pollute their
own bodies, reject authority and slander celestial be-
ings. But even the archangel Michael, when he was dis-
puting with the devil about the body of Moses, did not
dare to bring a slanderous accusation against him, but
said, 'The Lord rebuke you!' Yet these men speak abu-
sively against whatever they do not understand; and
what things they do understand by instinct, like un-
reasoning animals—these are the very things that destroy them.

"Woe to them! . . . They are clouds without rain,
blown along by the wind, autumn trees, without fruit
and uprooted—twice dead. They are wild waves of the
sea, foaming up their shame; wandering stars, for whom
blackest darkness has been reserved forever." (Jude 1:4–
12)

"Who is the liar? It is the man that denies Jesus is
the Christ. Such a man is the antichrist—he denies the
Father and the Son. No one who denies the Son has
the Father; whoever acknowledges the Son has the
Father also.

"See that what you have heard from the beginning
remains in you. If it does, you also will remain in the

Son and the Father. And this is what he promised us—even eternal life.

"I am writing these things to you about those who are trying to lead you astray. As for you, the anointing you received from him remains in you, and you do not need anyone to teach you. But as his anointing teaches you about all things and as that anointing is real, not counterfeit—just as it has taught you, remain in him." (1 John 2:22–27)

On the news today it was reported that some group was publishing a "gender neutral" Bible. How trendy. How P.C. It must be something to tell the god you want to worship how he or she is supposed to be and what they stand for and what they're capable of and what they have jurisdiction over.

Why don't we just carve an idol? Any god that takes orders from people isn't God. And any Bible that gets edited to someone's taste isn't the Bible. God is a *he* because He says so and if He changed himself to whatever form to tickle our sensibilities, He wouldn't be God. Come on! Don't call yourselves Christians. You are nothing but rebellious spirits who want salvation à la carte.

"Above all, you must understand that no prophecy of Scripture came about by the prophet's own interpretation. For prophecy never had its origin in the will of man, but men spoke from God as they were carried along by the Holy Spirit." (2 Peter 1:20–21)

Remember the plumb line in the book of Amos? Recognition and submission to the lordship of Jesus Christ is the plumb line to Christianity. We don't get to make Him into a girl or dress Him up and put funny hats on Him. Unbelievable. You're messing with the maker of heaven and earth! Surely you're not serious about any religion you make up for yourselves.

So what are Christians supposed to do in this day and time? The same as 2000 years ago.

> ". . . if my people, who are called by my name, will humble themselves and pray and seek my face and turn from their wicked ways, then will I hear from heaven and forgive their sin and will heal their land." (2 Chronicles 7:14)

Christians are called by His name. We are told to repent, humble ourselves, and pray.

> "Dear friends, I urge you as aliens and strangers in the world, to abstain from sinful desires, which war against your soul. Live such good lives among the pagans that, though they accuse you of doing wrong, they may see your good deeds and glorify God on the day he visits us." (1 Peter 2:11–12)

Live right and do right.

> "For this very reason, make every effort to add to your faith goodness; and to goodness, knowledge; and to knowledge, self-control; and to self-control, perseverance; and to perseverance, godliness; and to godliness, brotherly kindness; and to brotherly kindness, love. For if you possess these qualities in increasing measure,

they will keep you from being ineffective and unproductive in your knowledge of our Lord Jesus Christ." (2 Peter 1:5–8)

I'm one of those that think life today is pretty much the same as it always has been. The biological needs are the same. The basic motivations are the same. However, today and especially this century, mankind has been, for good and bad, avalanched with information. This does set us apart from previous generations. As Christians we literally have to guard our hearts and minds to what we and our family read, watch, and listen to. I'm not for censorship or for disconnecting the satellite dish and moving to Wyoming, though I would like to live there. What I'm saying is that there is much in the world that would separate us from Christ and that must be guarded against. The best way I know is to read the Bible every day, pray, and go to a good church. The Holy Spirit will guide us daily.

> "Therefore, my dear friends . . . continue to work out your salvation with fear and trembling, for it is God who works in you to will and to act according to his good purpose.
> "Do everything without complaining or arguing, so that you may become blameless and pure, children of God without fault in a crooked and depraved generation, in which you shine like stars in the universe as you hold out the word of life . . ." (Philippians 2:12–16)

So we must stop the sin that hinders us and separates us from God. We have to REMAIN in JESUS and grow as Christians.

"But our citizenship is in heaven. And we eagerly await a Savior from there, the Lord Jesus Christ, who, by the power that enables him to bring everything under his control, will transform our lowly bodies so that they will be like his glorious body." (Philippians 3:20–21)

"Rejoice in the Lord always. I will say it again: Rejoice! Let your gentleness be evident to all. The Lord is near. Do not be anxious about anything, but in everything, by prayer and petition, with thanksgiving, present your requests to God. And the peace of God, which transcends all understanding, will guard your hearts and your minds in Christ Jesus." (Philippians 4:4–7)

"I can do everything through him who gives me strength." (Philippians 4:13)

THE HOLY LAND

"Then you will know that I, the Lord your God, dwell in Zion, my holy hill. Jerusalem will be holy; never again will foreigners invade her." (Joel 3:17)

As it is written, Abraham had a son by Hagar, his wife's maidservant because his wife was barren. His name was Ishmael. Sarah, Abraham's wife, bore him a son, Isaac, fourteen years later. After this, she insisted that Abraham send Hagar and Ishmael away. This concerned Abraham:

"But God said to him, 'Do not be so distressed about the boy and your maidservant. Listen to whatever Sarah tells you, because it is through Isaac that your offspring will be reckoned. I will make the son of your maid-servant into a nation also, because he is your offspring.'" (Genesis 21:12–13)

Bear in mind those last two sentences.

> "These were the sons of Ishmael, and these are the
> names of the twelve tribal rulers according to their
> settlements and camps . . . His descendants settled in
> the area from Havilah to Shur, near the border of Egypt
> as you go toward Asshur. And they lived in hostility
> toward all their brothers." (Genesis 25:16–18)

These twelve tribal rulers, the sons of Ishmael, are the
twelve families of Arab tribes. Later, Isaac had two sons,
Jacob and Esau. It was Jacob who had twelve sons (see Genesis 35:21), and they are the twelve Jewish tribes. And it
was Jacob's sons who followed their brother Joseph into
Egypt, at first as honored guests of Pharaoh. As that generation passed away and the esteem of their brother Joseph
was forgotten, the respect for the Hebrew God faded. Then
the Egyptians enslaved the Jews. Seventy descendants of
Jacob traveled to Egypt but when God brought them out
400 years later they had become three million.

And it was those descendants of Abraham who had now
become a nation, that God would lead out of bondage with
Moses as their shepherd to the Promised Land. The land
He promised to Abraham, Isaac, and Jacob, that Moses be-
held before he died and Joshua entered into with the Israelites.

> "On that day the Lord made a covenant with Abram
> and said, 'To your descendants I give this land, from
> the river of Egypt to the great river, the Euphrates . . .'"
> (Genesis 15:18)

"Moses my servant is dead. Now then, you and all
these people, get ready to cross the Jordan River into the
land I am about to give to them—to the Israelites. I will
give you every place where you set your foot, as I promised Moses. Your territory will extend from the desert to
Lebanon, and from the great river, the Euphrates—all
the Hittite country—to the Great Sea on the west."
(Joshua 1:2–4)

God is saying that from the Nile east to the Euphrates,
west to the sea, and north to Lebanon belongs to Israel. The
capital is Jerusalem. The Israelites under Moses and then
Joshua (with divine power) conquered the land from the
Canaanites as God directed them. King David and his son
Solomon continued Israel's expansion by defeating the Phi-
listines. Approximately 950 B.C. the first temple was built
by King Solomon in Jerusalem. Israel drifted from God and
split into two kingdoms, Israel in the north and Judah in
the south. About 200 years later the Assyrians conquered
Israel. In 586 B.C. Babylon conquered Judah. Then the Persians conquered Babylon; then 200 years later Alexander
the Great conquered the Persians. After Alexander died,
Egypt and Syria were in control until the Romans rolled
into town taking Jerusalem in 63 B.C., holding it for about
400 years. Then the Byzantine Empire had its turn for about
300 years when they were kicked out by Muslims in 638
A.D. Muslims built the DOME OF THE ROCK AND AL-
AQSA MOSQUE ON TOP OF THE RUINS OF THE JEW-
ISH TEMPLE about fifty years later. Syria, Iraq, and Egypt
took turns administering the area until Christians during
the Crusades wrested it away for about 100 years until they

were in turn defeated by Saladin in 1187. Egypt controlled until 1516 when the Turks during the Ottoman Empire got their shot for about 400 years. World War I started and the Arabs revolted against the Turks. Then the British got involved and immigration of Jews back into Israel continued, actually having started in a big way in 1882, mostly from Eastern Europe.

As Jews continued to pour in and prosper, tensions mounted as various nations tried to get rid of the Jews, while clashes between Arab interests and the Zionists escalated. World War II came and went and there were massive diplomatic efforts and terrorism on both sides until in the spring of 1948 President Truman said that America will support the re-creation of Israel. And on May 14, 1948 at 4 P.M. in Tel Aviv, Israel was declared a nation again which President Truman promptly recognized. The following day Egypt, Syria, Lebanon, Jordan and Iraq attacked the fledgling nation from all sides. The military war was over about a year later and Israel still stood.

Later, after a series of Arab aggressions, Israel attacked the Egyptian Air Force in 1967 in a pre-emptive strike. Egypt had already moved its army into the Sinai desert and blockaded the Israeli port of Eilat. Egypt was joined again by Jordan, Syria, Lebanon and Iraq. They were defeated in six days.

Reading all this history (at which I am only a novice) I hope you see that this territory has been fought over ever since Israel was born and it is NOT about territory IT'S ABOUT WHOSE GOD IS THE TRUE GOD. Why else would they build a holy site ON TOP of the Jewish temple that pre-dated it by over 1,500 years? The other day nineteen Jews died as a suicide bomber murdered them on a Jerusalem bus. Now the descendants of proud Arab fighters wage a coward's war by blowing up civilians and crashing civilian planes into buildings. If Allah is God and you want Jerusalem then take it . . . but it's not time for that yet.

So what's going to happen? Do you know that the Jews are well on their way in preparation of rebuilding the temple? There is the special breed of red heifers now being raised in the U.S. which is the strain of cows that would be used if animal sacrifice was started again. Of course the temple would have to be re-built and all the articles of gold that were used to worship Jehovah in the first two temples would have to be re-created. Artisans are already hard at work on these. The priests of the Levite clan would have to be selected and trained too. That's underway as well. But again the temple would have to be rebuilt. To do that Al-Aqsa would have to be torn down which is supposedly smack dab on top of the temple ruins on the top of the hill and the Dome of the Rock to the south would have to go as well which is on the old courtyard area.

See many Jews believe that if the temple is rebuilt and daily sacrifices are renewed, the Messiah will come to Israel. As a Christian I don't agree with that at all. Most Jews don't believe the Messiah has come. As a Christian I know He has but will come again. Yet in a way I think the Jews are right about something. I agree that when the temple is rebuilt (and it will be) Jesus, the Messiah will come soon. Why? Because for that to happen the Jews will have to regain control of the Temple Mount and the structures, which the

Arabs regard as the third holiest in their faith, will have to be demolished.

Under present circumstances that would mean one heck of a war, but there is an interesting twist. When Israel was reborn in 1948 it controlled Jerusalem, but not the Old City where the Temple Mount is. The Old City was divided. After the Six-Day War, Israel gained control of ALL Jerusalem and ten days later they gave control of the Temple Mount TO THE MUSLIMS! Why didn't they tear down the Islamic structures and then build on top of them? The Muslims built on top of Jewish temple ruins. Today no Jew or Christian is allowed to pray or to carry a Bible or Torah on the Temple Mount, even if they're allowed in during visiting hours. It is patrolled by armed Arab guards who guard the entrance as well.

So here is the HOLIEST site to the Jews on land they reconquered given over to MUSLIM CONTROL. Since that time several attempts by Jewish zealots have been made to regain it. They've been stopped by the Arab guards and also THE ISRAELI ARMY. To add even more spice, many rabbis are glad Muslims control it. They don't believe any Jew should set foot on the Temple Mount because they are UNCLEAN. Muslims aren't?

Here's this roughly thirty-acre site that has fundamental importance to the world's three great monotheistic religions. Israel won it back and GAVE it away. Even though Israel controls the area all around the Temple Mount, they still allow themselves to be forbidden to even PRAY there. Why? REMEMBER JERUSALEM IS UNDER MONUMENTAL SUPERNATURAL INFLUENCE. Why did Israel give it back to the Muslims? Because God was in charge then and He is now and IT WASN'T TIME FOR ISRAEL TO HAVE IT YET.

This is what to look for. The Jews believe the Messiah will come and restore Israel, the temple, Mosaic law and bring peace to Israel. That would take one major miracle. I believe that Jesus IS and WAS and WILL BE THE MESSIAH. HE WILL COME BACK NOT TO RE-INSTITUTE MOSAIC LAW BUT TO FULFILL IT, SINCE WE CAN'T FULFILL THE LAW. YET HE IS OUR BLOOD SACRIFICE, SO WE CAN STEP ON THE TEMPLE MOUNT AND ENTER RIGHT INTO THE HOLY OF HOLIES AND FALL RIGHT DOWN AT THE FEET OF GOD! No unclean person could do this. The Jews are right here, but what they don't accept is that ONLY BY THE BLOOD OF JESUS can we do it.

So Jesus will come back but first a false messiah will appear. I believe the antichrist will come first. (Read Daniel and Revelation)

He will be part of a ten-nation confederation that has seven leaders of which he is one. He will suffer a terrible head wound but will miraculously recover. He will have extraordinary charisma and will pretend to be a man of peace. He will strike a seven-year deal. Three-and-a-half years into it, he will end daily sacrifices. He will be joined by the false prophet who will perform great miracles and demand that an image of the beast be set up and worshipped in the temple 1290 days after sacrifice has stopped (Daniel chapter 12).

I'm no prophet. All this is clearly in the Bible. See Daniel 8:23–27, 11:35–45, and Revelation 13:1–18 to read about the antichrist and the false prophet.

"While I was speaking and praying, confessing my sin and the sin of my people Israel and making my request to the Lord my God for his holy hill—while I was still in prayer, Gabriel, the man I had seen in the earlier vision, came to me in swift flight about the time of the evening sacrifice. He instructed me and said to me 'Daniel, I have now come to you to give you insight and understanding. As soon as you began to pray, an answer was given, which I have come to tell you, for you are highly esteemed. Therefore consider the message and understand the vision:

"Seventy 'sevens' are decreed for your holy people and your holy city to finish transgression, to put an end to sin, to atone for wickedness, to bring in everlasting righteousness, to seal up vision and prophecy and to anoint the most holy.

"Know and understand this: From the issuing of the decree to restore and rebuild Jerusalem until the Anointed One, the ruler, comes, there will be seven 'sevens' and sixty-two 'sevens'. It will be rebuilt with streets and a trench, but in times of trouble. After the sixty-two 'sevens', the Anointed One will be cut off and have nothing. The people of the ruler who will come will destroy the city and the sanctuary. The end will come like a flood. War will continue until the end, and desolations have been decreed. He will confirm a covenant with many for one 'seven'. In the middle of the 'seven' he will put an end to sacrifice and offering. And on a wing of the temple he will set up an abomination that causes desolation, until the end that is decreed is poured out on him."
(Daniel 9:20–27)

Many preachers don't believe the Bible really means this. Others believe the "abomination that causes desolation" happened when the Roman general Titus destroyed the second temple in A.D. 70. Later, Antiochus Epiphanes in A.D. 167 desecrated the temple ruins and had a statue of Jupiter erected on the altar site and had sacrifices offered to it.

"Don't let anyone deceive you in any way, for that day will not come until the rebellion occurs and the man of lawlessness is revealed, the man doomed to destruction. He will oppose and exalt himself over everything that is called God or is worshiped, so that he sets himself up in God's temple, proclaiming himself to be God.

"Don't you remember that when I was with you I used to tell you these things? And now you know what is holding him back, so that he may be revealed at the proper time. For the secret power of lawlessness is already at work; but the one who now holds it back will continue to do so till he is taken out of the way. And then the lawless one will be revealed, whom the Lord Jesus will overthrow with the breath of his mouth and destroy by the splendor of his coming. The coming of the lawless one will be in accordance with the work of Satan displayed in all kinds of counterfeit miracles, signs and wonders, and in every sort of evil that deceives those who are perishing. They perish because they refused to love the truth and so be saved." (2 Thessalonians 2:3–10)

Remember that much of the Old Testament was prophecy for the days after it and still yet to come. Much of it mirrors and parallels the New Testament and the days yet to come.

> "The beast which you saw, once was, now is not, and will come up out of the Abyss and go to his destruction. The inhabitants of the earth whose names have not been written in the book of life from the creation of the world will be astonished when they see the beast, because he once was, now is not, and yet will come." (Revelation 17:8)

I used to strongly feel that whoever the antichrist is, it would have to be a Jew or to appear as one because the majority of Jews will have to accept him. Reading the above suggests to me that some prominent historical figure, alive and dead before the disciple John's time, (he wrote Revelation) will be brought back to life. Whoever this is will somehow gain enormous power as head of a ten-nation confederation and will make a seven-year deal with the Jews to allow the rebuilding of the temple and the re-establishment of the daily sacrifice. Then 3 1/2 years later, he will break his covenant when he will be revealed for who he truly is.

> And all Christians will be called away: "For the Lord himself will come down from heaven, with a loud command, with the voice of the archangel and with the trumpet call of God, and the dead in Christ shall rise first. After that, we who are still alive and are left will be caught

up together with them in the clouds to meet the Lord in the air. And so we will be with the Lord forever." (1 Thessalonians 4:16–17) (The Rapture)

"After this I looked and there before me was a great multitude that no one could count, from every nation, tribe, people, and language, standing before the throne and in front of the Lamb . . ." (Revelation 7:9)

As this happens 144,000 Jews will be sealed, 12,000 from each of the twelve tribes which will accept Jesus as their Messiah (Revelation 7:1–8). Then the Tribulation begins:

"Then I heard a loud voice from the temple saying to the seven angels, 'Go, pour out the seven bowls of God's wrath on the earth.'" (Revelation 16:1) Read Revelation 16:1–21

"Then they gathered the kings together to the place that in Hebrew is called Armageddon." (Revelation 16:16)

"I saw heaven standing open and there before me was a white horse, whose rider is called Faithful and True. With justice he judges and makes war. His eyes are like blazing fire, and on his head are many crowns. He has a name written on him that no one knows but he himself. He is dressed in a robe dipped in blood, and his name is the Word of God. The armies of heaven were following him . . ." (Revelation 19:11–14)

The rider is Jesus of course.

"And I saw an angel standing in the sun, who cried in a loud voice to all the birds flying in midair, 'Come, gather together for the great supper of God, so that you may eat the flesh of kings, generals, and mighty men, of horses and their riders, and the flesh of all people, free and slave, small and great.'

"Then I saw the beast and the kings of the earth and their armies gathered together to make war against the rider on the horse and his army. But the beast was captured, and with him the false prophet who had performed the miraculous signs on his behalf. With these signs he had deluded those who had received the mark of the beast and worshiped his image. The two of them were thrown alive into the fiery lake of burning sulfur. The rest of them were killed with the sword that came out of the mouth of the rider on the horse, and all the birds gorged themselves on their flesh." (Revelation 19:17–21)

Just as God has His holy trinity, God, the Father; Jesus, the Son; and the Holy Spirit, Satan will establish a counterfeit satanic trinity. Satan himself will be its head, with the antichrist, "the son of perdition"; and the false prophet. So we see that Jesus will return with the armies of heaven and will dispose of the antichrist and the false prophet. Then Satan, himself, is taken care of.

"And I saw an angel coming down out of heaven, having the key to the Abyss and holding in his hand a great chain. He seized the dragon, that ancient serpent, who is the devil, or Satan, and bound him for a thousand years." (Revelation 20:1–2)

Then Christ reigns on earth for a thousand years. When the millennium is up, Satan is released and goes out to deceive the world again. The armies he gathers are defeated by fire from heaven then he and his followers are tossed into the burning lake of sulfur. Read Revelation 20:4–10.

"If anyone's name was not found written in the book of life, he was thrown into the lake of fire." (Revelation 20:15)

PLEASE take this to heart. READ the Bible for yourself. PRAY for WISDOM. The point that people miss, including many intellectual preachers, is that they are LIMITING GOD BY THEIR OWN LOGIC AND TEACHING and when is GOD bound by that? The ones who say it has already happened seem to miss that Jesus and the armies of heaven have NOT come back yet and Satan IS still very powerful. These learned prophets see past and over and around the Bible, the foundation of the very faith they profess. And the COMPROMISERS and the fools who say this is all just figurative speech are just tired men who have too much of the world and are scared to get and stay close enough to God to be who they could be. And the Jews who admiringly reverence the HOLINESS of God so that they believe only the sanctified high priest can enter into the HOLY of HOLIES miss that JESUS IS BOTH THE HIGH PRIEST AND THE

SANCTIFICATION SO HE INDEED FULFILLS THE
PROPHETS AND THE LAW!

And it is this Jesus who reconciles you and me, just everyday sinners to God! Don't swallow the wisdom of the world without giving Jesus a chance. I know it seems like God is dead. I know it looks like if He isn't, He must not care, but I promise you, give Him a chance and He'll show you He's very much alive. Then read the Bible and cling to its truth. Yield to its teaching and give Jesus a chance. Don't blindly accept what any man says. The power of God will come into your life and you'll see what's going on in Israel is the same thing that's going on around the world, in your neighborhood and with you and with me. That is the WAR between GOD and the enemies of GOD. The Holy Land is special because it is marked territory.

The other day terrorists blew up an Israeli bus then machine-gunned the survivors. I missed the international outcry. Then Israel attacked the home of a known Hamas leader killing him and innocents, including children and the outcry was immediate. Israel apologized for the loss of innocent life. The point is they kill Jews and anyone (remember 9/11) indiscriminately. When Arab gunmen attack Jewish settlers they don't just shoot the adults. They kill the kids too. Surely a dead Arab child is just as dead as a dead Jewish child or a dead American one, BUT Israel will try not to kill innocents and neither does America but the terrorists don't care, and the international community HATES Israel because God is behind her. That little country that causes so much trouble, that if it weren't for its few friends (and God himself) would have already been reduced to rubble for good and wouldn't be such a pain in the tail for the world.

Let us understand that GOD is a pain for the world because HE won't let the world do as it pleases; Israel is a pain because God has chosen her to be HIS. This is why Israel has been reduced to rubble time and time again and why the JEWS have been persecuted all through time and why the WORLD will soon welcome the antichrist because he will project a solution for the WORLD to the problem of Israel and the Jews. The Bible has told us what will happen.

The situation in Israel seems to get worse every day. No nation could withstand such a constant terror barrage without soon saying, "Enough!" It could blow wide open any day. And we have defeated Iraq. God was with us. Reportedly, Saddam could have had nuclear weapons capability in three years. What do YOU think will happen now that it's over? Like after the Gulf War, Arab opportunists will go at Israel, but this time Saudi Arabia and other Arab countries will help us minimally, if at all. So I believe in the near future after much unrest, the antichrist will be seen as a man of peace who will most probably gain Jewish control of the Temple Mount in exchange for land for a Palestinian state with no or diminishing Jewish control. Most Jews have been readily willing to give up land for peace, but they have seen it spat back in their face. The Temple Mount would do it. The Palestinians dream of a nation without Israeli control. Arab interests may be satisfied if their land included Hebron where the tomb of the patriarchs is. Remember the displaced Palestinians have long been a problem for them. However I believe some Arabs have only used the Palestinians as a way to fight Israel. Of course for some Arabs it will be another period to sharpen their knives and for some Jews they will look eagerly to the arrival of a war-like messiah, but most people on both sides will enjoy a short-lived peace.

Which brings us to the latest diplomatic effort. On April 30, 2003, on the same day the new Palestinian Prime Minister Mahmoud Abbas was sworn in, the "Road Map to Peace" was presented both to Mr. Abbas and Israeli Prime Minister Ariel Sharon. A collaborative effort produced by the United States, the European Union, the United Nations and Russia, it calls for Israeli withdrawal from Palestinian towns, the dismantling of Jewish settlements constructed after 2001, an immediate cease-fire, and the establishment of a Palestinian state, most likely two to three years from now. On the same day a homicide bomber linked to Mr. Abbas killed three at a popular bar in Tel Aviv and wounded fifty-five.

So we see a concerted plan for a Palestinian state. The tricky part is what exactly will be its borders? Will the Jews regain the Temple Mount in the initial plan? You know the Arabs want Jerusalem as the capital of Palestine, and Israel and her few allies won't let that happen. Of course, if the truth were totally known, the Arab extremists don't want just a Palestinian state, they want the destruction of Israel. (It doesn't matter how much ransom the kidnapper is paid, he wants to kill anyway.) My gut tells me that the terrorists won't stop, so this "Road Map" won't truly be fulfilled until after some significant military action between Israel and her hostile neighbors. When the dust clears, the Arabs will be humbled enough to give up the Temple Mount and the international pressure and desperation of the Israeli people for peace will push Israel to concede precious land for an unfettered Palestinian state. This is when the ten-nation confederation will step in.

So who will comprise this ten-nation confederation? Let's look at the players who are now involved in laying out this "Road Map" and the others on the board and their affiliations. The U.N. Security Council has fifteen members, five of which are permanent. NATO has nineteen members. The Arab League has twenty-two (Interestingly one of its founding principles was the prevention of a Jewish state in Israel . . . HELLO . . .). The European Union currently has fifteen members and ten more countries have been invited to join. Whoever it will be, its organization will have the muscle and influence to rule most of the world for a time, which leads me to believe most of Europe has to be involved.

This agrees with most interpretations of King Nebuchadnezzar's dream described in the second chapter of Daniel, of the great statue made of gold (representing Babylon), silver (Medo-Persia), bronze (Greece), iron (Rome) and ending with feet and toes of baked clay and iron. Historically, we're down to the feet and toes, which descend from what used to be the Roman Empire, which at its height encompassed North Africa, almost all of Europe, up into Britain and some of the Middle East. In Revelation the beast with seven heads represents the seven hills of where the woman sits and also seven kings, of which the antichrist will be the eighth. The blasphemous little horn in Daniel chapter 7 is one horn from a ten-horned beast (just like Revelation 17's seven-headed, ten-horned beast); we're told in Daniel that three of the first horns were uprooted before it.

So the Bible suggests strongly that this ten-nation con-federation which the antichrist will gain control of, will be geographically centered literally where Rome stood (Europe). His country will control or absorb three of the original ten nations of this confederation and he will lead it.

The very interesting part of what's happening in world politics now are the rifts in the U.N. Security Council and also in NATO, led mainly by France. Of course Chirac and France have long been business partners with Iraq, but even more so it seems that some countries are tired of standing in America's shadow. Russia longs for the power she once had. So how united will NATO remain? The U.N. has proven to be a good idea but spineless. We'll also see more Muslim monarchies weakened as their more radical citizens rebel as they see their leaders in bed with the infidels. An impotent U.N., a fractured NATO and a de-stabilized Middle East prepare the ground for a larger war which will involve Israel, but will NOT be the final battle. The antichrist will be seen as a great peacemaker and as the head of the ten nations, will deceitfully bring peace to Israel, offering the seven-year deal. Israel will begin making daily sacrifices and half-way into it the liar will break the deal and turn on Israel. I believe this is when all Christians will be raptured. The false prophet will appear and order an image of the beast be made and worshipped in the temple. The 144,000 Jews will be sealed by God, accept Jesus and be the remnant saved from Israel. The antichrist and false prophet will require the mark of the beast for all commerce and whoever receives the mark or worships the beast will face the wrath of God.

There will be a great revival in America, yet there will also be a great falling away as good and evil struggle for our souls. Good is stronger but God has made it our choice. I'm sickened at the number of kidnappings and rapes and murders of children we've seen lately. Satan is stepping it up in an attempt to frighten and disillusion us. It will get worse as we endure and focus on Israel for what will surely come.

So who am I and what do I know? I'm nobody. Just a regular person like you, but I KNOW that GOD IS and I BELIEVE the BIBLE. I know what God has shown me and I know that for HIS reasons I've worked on this while HE's worked on me for about seven years now. All I want is for anyone who is not SAVED to be saved. So all I pray is that people give Jesus a chance. Don't blindly swallow the junk this world throws at you. Eternity for you and most likely the ones you love (since you influence your family and friends) is at stake, and I'M NOT OVERSTATIN' IT!

Pray. Find a Bible and read any part of it you want. Then take some quiet time and think. Let God speak to you. Go to church. Talk to a Christian. Go to a courtroom or an ER or a maternity ward or a PRISON. LIFE. DEATH. MIRACLES. A FORGIVEN PAST. WHO DO YOU WANT TO BE NOW? AND WHERE DO YOU WANT TO BE LATER?

Israel is marked territory. You wanna know why?

"Jerusalem will be a city without walls. . . . And I myself will be a wall of fire around it,' declares the Lord, 'and I will be its glory within." (Zechariah 2:4–5)

"I am going to make Jerusalem a cup that sends all the surrounding peoples reeling. Judah will be besieged as well as Jerusalem. On that day when all the nations of the earth are gathered against her, I will make Jerusalem an immovable rock for all the nations." (Zechariah 12:2–3)

"'I am very jealous for Zion; I am burning with jealousy for her.' This is what the Lord says: 'I will return to Zion and dwell in Jerusalem. Then Jerusalem will be called the City of Truth, and the mountain of the Lord Almighty will be called the Holy Mountain.'

"This is what the Lord Almighty says: 'Once again men and women of ripe old age will sit in the streets of Jerusalem, each with cane in hand because of his age. The city streets will be filled with boys and girls playing there.'

"This is what the Lord Almighty says: 'It may seem marvelous to the remnant of this people at that time, but will it seem marvelous to me?' declares the Lord Almighty.

"This is what the Lord Almighty says: 'I will save my people from the countries of the east and the west. I will bring them back to live in Jerusalem; they will be my people, and I will be faithful and righteous to them as their God.'

"This is what the Lord Almighty says: 'You who now hear these words spoken by the prophets who were there when the foundation was laid for the house of the Lord Almighty, let your hands be strong so that the temple may be built." (Zechariah 8:2–9)

"On that day there will be no light, no cold nor frost. It will be a unique day, without daytime or night-time—a day known to the Lord. When evening comes, there will be light.

"On that day living water will flow out from Jerusalem, half to the eastern sea and half to the western sea, in summer and in winter.

"The Lord will be king over the whole earth. On that day there will be one Lord, and his name the only name." (Zechariah 14:6–9)

"And on that day there will no longer be a Canaanite in the house of the Lord Almighty." (Zechariah 14:21)

As much as it seems that the world is out of control, it's not. God is very much in control of everything. As insane as the situation seems in the Holy Land, God has HIS timetable. I want you to understand WHY that area is special. YOU are special too, and you'll have to make a choice. Listen to your heart. You know where you belong.

"The Lord bless you and keep you; the Lord make his face shine upon you and be gracious to you; the Lord turn his face toward you and give you peace." (Numbers 6:24–26)

"This is what the Lord Almighty says: 'Administer true justice; show mercy and compassion to one another. Do not oppress the widow or the fatherless, the alien or the poor, in your hearts do not think evil of each other.'" (Zechariah 7:9–10)

"'These are the things you are to do: Speak the truth to each other, and render true and sound judgment in your courts; do not plot evil against your neighbor, and do not love to swear falsely. I hate all this,' declares the Lord." (Zechariah 8:16–17)

"Jesus replied: 'Love the Lord your God with all your heart and with all your soul and with all your mind.' This is the first and greatest commandment. And the second is like it: 'Love your neighbor as yourself.' All the Law and the Prophets hang on these two commandments." (Matthew 22:37–40)

The Lord sees you and hears you and will bless you if you come to Him. May He bless you and your household. Amen, amen and amen.

Verse

JESUS

He knows all our problems.
He knows all our pain.
Through all of our hurt and tears
His Love still remains.

More precious than gold
And stronger than steel
His Blood bought our freedom
By a three-day march through Hell.

Wonderful Warrior,
My Savior and my Lord,
Illuminate the earth
With the Power of Your Word.

HOLY SPIRIT

Gift from God,
I am but a new wineskin
Yearning to be filled with new wine.
I have tasted You
And now can settle for nothing less.
Fill me, wash over me and run
Through me,
So that I can never be my old self
Again.

GOD

Father, how strong Your shoulders must be
To bear the weight of the world.
How big Your heart is to restore its Love.

What's it like to know so much
About so many?
So much knowledge You'd
Rather not know . . . but
Yet enough goodness, so
You can smile through Your tears.

Father, Your Power is too magnificent,
Too awesome for me to comprehend,
But Your Love I know well,
Your voice I run to
And Your laugh I delight in.

What's it like to look through the stars
At the earth below?
Moon-washed mountain peaks,
Twinkling city lights, sirens
And baby cries.

Father, may the world know You.
May everyone know the Truth
And run to it
And follow its familiar voice
Calling us home.

FINAL THOUGHTS

A good church is like a battery charger. Find a church that preaches the Bible, not one that they've written—THE Bible—and submit to God's authority in your life. If you're going somewhere that tells you not to change or surrender your control to God; you're wasting your time. God is POWER and if you'll submit to Him He WILL CHANGE YOUR LIFE.

For us Christians: Let us not fool ourselves and hold on to old sin habits. God will forgive us if we stumble, but if we continue to stick a toe in the mud when nobody's looking we're fooling ourselves. We are NEW creations and don't need to go back and put on our DEATH clothes. GOD SEES EVERYTHING. If we're on a path filled with snares and potholes, riddled with SIN TRAPS, we need to clear the trail or get on the right path.

As Americans it's hard to stay morally focused because in our popular culture almost everything's OK. We have to remember that GOD'S TRUTH is what matters and JESUS is our plumb line. WE can't go by MTV standards and be Christians or by popular standards that change with self-indulgent fashions and appetites that are set by human understanding.

GOD'S TRUTH IS ETERNAL AND NEVER CHANGES. Father, give US the strength to stay focused and obedient. Amen.

Suggested reading: The book of Genesis
The book of John
The book of Isaiah
The book of Romans
The rest of the Bible
The Pursuit of God by A.W. Tozer

To order additional copies of

GOD is ALIVE

Have your credit card ready and call:

1-877-421-READ (7323)

or please visit our web site at
www.pleasantword.com

Also available at: www.amazon.com
& www.barnesandnoble.com

Printed in the United States
1310800001B/163-210